Peter O'Connor was born in M[...]
graduate of Melbourne University, he w[...]
Director of Counselling at the Marriage Guidance Council of
Victoria. In 1972 he was awarded a Winston Churchill
Fellowship and completed his Ph.D. in Marriage and Family
Counselling at the University of Southern California. He has
held several academic and clinical appointments both here and
overseas, and he now practises in Melbourne. He is also the
author of *Mirror on Marriage* (1973), *Understanding Jung*
(1985) and *Dreams and the Search for Meaning* (1986).

By the same author

MIRROR ON MARRIAGE (1973)
UNDERSTANDING JUNG (1985)
DREAMS AND THE SEARCH FOR
MEANING (1986)

UNDERSTANDING
THE
MID-LIFE CRISIS

**DR PETER
O'CONNOR**

SUN
AUSTRALIA

First published 1981 by The Macmillan Company of Australia Pty Ltd
This edition published by Pan Macmillan Publishers Australia
a division of Pan Macmillan Australia Pty Limited
63-71 Balfour Street, Chippendale, Sydney
A.C.N. 001 184 014

Reprinted 1982, 1983, 1985, 1987, 1988, 1989, 1990, 1991

National Library of Australia
cataloguing-in-publication data:

O'Connor, Peter A.
Understanding the mid-life crisis.

Includes index
ISBN 0 7251 0374 4

1. Middle aged men. I. Title

155.6'32

Typeset in 11/12 point Baskerville
Printed in Australia by The Book Printer

To my children,
Felicity,
Elizabeth and
Patrick,
who serve to remind me of
life's unfolding pattern.

'My friend, a man's success or
failure is always with his own
Soul.'

A.E. (George Russell)

Contents

Acknowledgements

In writing this book I have been influenced by several people, although most of them were unaware of this. Friendship was, and is, a critical factor, one that sustained me through the difficult periods before I could manage to write this book, and continues beyond its completion. For this I have Chris and Geoff Minter to thank, simply for making friendship possible in a way that allowed me to feel more complete. To my colleague and close friend Bill Healy I also owe a debt of thanks for the endless hours of conversation and mutual concern that we have shared.

Joan Belcher has also been influential in the writing of this book and I take this opportunity of expressing my gratitude to her for the guidance and care she has given me. Glenda Banks, formerly of the *New Idea* magazine, Australia, and now feature journalist with the Herald and Weekly Times, Melbourne, was always willing to listen to my views and constantly to make written sense of them. It was she who provided the initial impetus for this book, since following a newspaper article she wrote on the male mid-life crisis, many men wrote to me about their own situation. I would also like to thank Dr Raynor Johnson, who was specifically influential in introducing me to the work of the Irish mystic and poet, A.E. (George Russell), and in sustaining my interest in Jung and the inner world.

Marjorie Newbold warrants my special thanks, since it was following her kind and characteristically unobtrusive offer to do some typing for me that I was able to find the necessary motivation to commence writing. Her willingness and competence in typing the manuscript have been of immense value to me.

My wife, Margaret, has been my strongest supporter and critic, both tasks having been undertaken with kindness and love. This is no mean achievement, since living with someone who is writing is a severe test of tolerance, loyalty and affection.

Finally, to the men with whom I had the privilege of talking, I record my deepest gratitude. They should consider this book their contribution — my pen was simply an instrument.

Preface 1987

This current reprint of *Understanding the Mid-Life Crisis* is the fourth. Seven years have elapsed since I first wrote the book. Apart from seven years being a significant number in itself, indicating a specific phase of life, this reprint seemed to demand some additional comments.

From simple beginnings in my own psyche the book has taken on a life of its own. Throughout the past seven years I have received numerous letters from readers which, almost without exception, have reflected and commented upon how the book spoke to them personally. Most of the people who have written to me expressed the relief that they derived from the book, since for them it put some sort of order into what was previously experienced as chaos. This feedback has been very rewarding, but I think more importantly that it confirms what I have already written — that is, that men, in particular, have been damaged by a tyranny of privacy that has negated the possibility of knowing the extent of the experiences they may share as individuals. That this book seems to speak personally to each man indicates that below the superficial level of our material being lies a vast common ground. The sharing of the mid-life experience, through recognition of this common ground, is clearly the way in which men can both explore, understand and grow from it.

The sharing provides for the possibility of curtailing, or at the very least, challenging, the more destructive and alienating qualities in males to pursue certainty only and eschew the realm of the uncertain. This theme appears again and again in my own private psychotherapy practice. Men seek help with the false hope that I will give definitive answers, when in fact the help lies in their learning to explore their own uncertainties. Mid-life is a profoundly disturbing time which serves to challenge our fixed beliefs and expose us to the fertile ground of 'not-knowing' — where imaginative, rather than rational thought resides. This restoration of the imaginal world reconnects a man to his inner self and this reconnection represents the healing from mid-life anxieties and depression.

What I could not have anticipated when I wrote the book was the response it would receive from women. Some were disappointed that I had only written about men, however the book was based on my interviews with men, not women, and I thought it was high time that a book was written for men. Other women have expressed gratitude that the book has provided them with a mechanism for speaking and relating to men about issues which previously they were not able to communicate. In particular they have found the book useful in opening up discussion about feelings.

Finally there is a group of women who have experienced confusion upon reading the book. This confusion has come from the fact that although the book is concerned with the male mid-life crisis, they found themselves heavily identifying with most of the material in it. How can they, as females, be having a male mid-life crisis? The answer, in part, is that by and large these are women who have spent the first half of their lives developing their careers. Hence they have struggled with and developed similar aspects of their personality to males. The development of competence in the outer world, the pursuit of success and power often require some diminution or under-development of the inner world, regardless of whether one is male or female. Thus one of the effects of the women's movement has been that there now exists a whole generation of women who have experienced the freedom to choose which aspects of their personalities they may develop in the first half of life. This group are now moving into the mid-life transitional period and are finding that they are experiencing very similar feelings to their male colleagues. particularly in the occupational sphere. Behind this is the same issue as for males, the urging from within oneself to begin the task of developing the inner world of feelings and imagination as the necessary task of the second half of life.

I hope that this reprint continues to bring to the readers, both male and female, some understanding and order into the critical experience of mid-life.

Peter A. O'Connor
Melbourne
1987

An Introduction

In late 1974 I returned from the USA to Australia after an absence of three years. I was then 32 and ostensibly had the proverbial 'world at my feet'. Here I was with a brand-new, shiny Ph.D., all ready to take off and play a major role in the Australian community — at least that was my fantasy. Why then did I feel a pang, a constant, nagging, low level, dull, throbbing ache inside my psyche? 'It's just resettling pains', and 'I must be suffering from readjustment tension', were the type of thoughts I mustered in order to reassure and comfort myself. Such thoughts were aided and abetted in their capacity to deceive by the socially acceptable analgesics of fervent activity and self-constructed tasks of importance.

A year elapsed and I resigned from my counselling position to take up a university lectureship. I was pursuing the thought that if I were involved in a university setting I would experience the stimulation and challenge that I had now convinced myself were missing. 'Yes, that's all it is, just a lack of stimulation and opportunity to fully utilize what I consider to be my talents', and 'I am really an academic, a researcher, not a clinician': on and on went my justification and explanation of the underlying sense of malaise that I felt, the horrible, nagging sense of uselessness, and the even more horrible vision of it all being a tragic game of charades. Was I playing a game of charades, a tragic though socially acceptable one, or was it that once again in my life I was simply out of step? I had failed miserably in my attempts to become a boy scout, being dismissed for unruly behaviour; I had been dishonourably discharged from the school cadets for persistent absence without leave: was this the same pattern over again?

These fears received increasing confirmation when within three months of changing positions my inner sense of uneasiness and anxiety was markedly heightened. Again I resorted to internal explanations: was I simply difficult if not impossible to please? Other people seemed able to accept what I regarded as intolerable mediocrity. Were my standards unrealistic? Did I expect a perfect world? Was I maladjusted? Here I was earning a more than respectable salary in a more than respectable position at an established university! By all reports, including those of eternally critical students, I was giving from moderately good to excellent lectures, and to all appearances I was well suited to being an academic. Only from my behaviour in meetings did colleagues catch a glimpse of the unruly boy scout, but such behaviour was swiftly and silently labelled 'eccentric', a euphemism of unending popularity in universities. This convenient label hid from myself and my colleagues the ever-increasing pain and bitterness of disillusion; the horror and shock felt when a fantasy you have been protected by is shattered.

My anxiety and pervasive sense of loss and aimlessness were accompanied by the ever-present intellectual prosthesis of such thoughts as 'Education is passé, students only want a meal ticket.' I protected myself from the full impact of nihilism by developing the idea of my having something valuable to offer but it being the wrong time and place: 'Universities are just intellectual supermarkets'; 'intellectual and true scholastic endeavour are a thing of the past'. It is relatively easy for such sentiments to provide a permanent shelter from the persistent sense of futility.

However, for me they only provided overnight accommodation from my inner sense of uselessness and I increasingly felt a sense of detachment as if the 'world was all out there' and I very separate and disconnected from it. I had two motor car accidents within a period of one month which led me to wonder whether I had unwittingly or unconsciously brought them about. Did I want to destroy myself and avoid the constant sense of boredom with much of life – a life that others seemed to find satisfying? Would I finally just give up the struggle to find some sense of meaning and accept the status quo as others did? Would I finally accept that the struggle was pointless and that hoping for meaning and satisfaction was an adolescent fantasy, replete with unattainable idealism? This vision of blackness was only occasionally broken by my escape into the idea that perhaps I ought to resign and try writing full time, then I would be free; but would I? Did I, in fact, have anything to write about? My feelings of insecurity and the unrealistic aspects of such a solution crowded in, forcing it back into the realm of the impossible. This idea nevertheless became a fairly repetitive one over time and served the purpose of providing an escape hatch from the omnipresent sense of hopelessness.

But the predominant feeling was one of resentment, unadulterated bitter resentment, coupled with a feeling of powerlessness and frustration. It was as if one were a marionette, moving to the strings of an unseen puppeteer. I had a tendency to seek explanations which were external to myself and to refuse to recognize that the strings and puppeteer were within. Alongside this very personal confusion was the irony that I, as a psychologist and counsellor, was supposed to know about such matters; the adage 'physician heal thyself' took on an ominous quality of reality. But what was it that I was to heal myself of, if indeed healing was what was needed? There were no obvious symptoms – some tangible physical manifestation of the inner disease would have been a welcome relief from the turmoil. By outside standards, by other standards, I was successful; but to me the clarion of success only served to intensify my inner sense of emptiness. It was as if my success had brought in its wake failure, and although it was painful to be a failure, at least it meant there was still the goal of success to strive for, providing a temporary distraction from feelings of emptiness. Achieving success, however, only leaves you with the goal of failure, a painful paradox that I was unable to resolve. Success seemed to bring into stark relief

3

one's sense of failure and inadequacy: is it therefore any wonder that we continue to strive?

I became increasingly preoccupied in my professional life with the seemingly flippant and cynical task of producing a theory of failing, that is, helping to articulate the nature of successful failing. At the same time I became interested in the topics of death and grieving. In retrospect it is very clear that these so-called professional and objective interests were external manifestations of my inner world. I was grieving on the inside, mourning for the loss of purpose, and yet at that time to be experiencing grief was an absurd notion which made no sense at the conscious intellectual level.

As so often happens when we feel anxious and experience conflict, we imagine that we alone are experiencing these feelings. We have produced for ourselves a tyranny of privacy wherein it is regarded as totally unacceptable to share our uncertainties, our fears, our chaos, for to do so would expose us as inadequate. I felt all of this pressure and even as I write now I feel it once again. We seem to have some agreement whereby we maintain the illusion of adequacy, however much it is in actuality lacking: a complicity of competence. The rules are clear: 'You can only be inadequate if we can label you as disturbed or insane (in university circles eccentric!); otherwise show and claim only competence and do not dare to blow our cover'! Gradually I gained confidence in the idea of competence being a hoax and incompetence, with glimpses of competence, being the reality. Two other factors fed in here; one was my well-developed inclination for playing the role of exposing the emperor and informing all within earshot that he had no clothes on. The other factor was my personal commitment, which formed the hard core of my professional practice, to the idea that it was obligatory to reflect, and to share these reflections with others: to share with each other our uncertainties as well as our certainties.

Yet despite these two factors it was very difficult to escape the feeling of 'being silly'. However, increasingly I listened to friends and colleagues and sensed that I was not alone! There was some confirmation of my ideas. Hesitatingly I explored, shared some of my confusion. Yes! Further confirmation. I

4

began to experience a growing confidence that my personal reactions were shared by several male friends and colleagues, that somehow I, in my individual psyche, had captured a general process of the male psyche — at least in those psyches around 35 years of age! For it seemed that many men of this age were also feeling a pervasive sense of futility and a sense of terror at the thought of the next 30 years being a continual repetition, like a well-worn re-run of their current situation. Marriage break-ups, affairs and separations were a fairly common occurrence, some expected, some unexpected. Above all else it became clear that some phenomenon of considerable force was occurring in each of our lives with noticeable regularity, even if it were played out in a variety of ways. Whilst the lyrics varied between individuals, the notes of depression, loss and purposelessness remained constant.

Around this time I was invited to give a public lecture to a symposium on family life which had the general theme of how to live a happier, more satisfying life with each other. Increasingly, consistent with my own sense of resentment, I was becoming irritated with what I felt to be the 'goodie goodie', revamped 'holier than thou' type of attitude that was frequently to be found in bodies or organizations concerned with the family.

Despite my irritation, the internal pressure to reflect upon and make sense of my inner difficulties and confusion led me to accept the invitation, since I perceived it as an opportunity to collect my thoughts. I had by now developed the habit of trying to put down on paper what I was struggling with at any time, and not infrequently these jottings found their way into a lecture. Thus I produced a lecture on what came to be described as 'family life stages' for this symposium. The central theme of the lecture was separation, beginning with the foetus separating from the womb, continuing through the separation of children going to school, through adolescence, to their separation from the family, and finally ending up with the separation of the parents themselves through death, or, as is the case in an ever-increasing number of families, through divorce. In this lecture I proposed that we could make better sense of our experience of family life

5

if we thought of it in terms of a succession of losses with the accompanying feeling of grief. This theme was fast capturing and making sense of my inner world and, although it might first appear a somewhat cynical, pessimistic view, it seemed to make sense to others.

However, my original thought about there being a recognizable pattern of disillusion in males around 35 years of age, continued to press in on me. I was now convinced of its existence beyond my personal boundaries and another invitation to give a lecture, this time to a professional audience, provided a further opportunity for exploration. Despite considerable uncertainty on my part I decided to place the major emphasis in the lecture on the phase in the family when a man was passing through this now identifiable phase of massive uncertainty and confusion. In short, I decided to concentrate on what I had now come to know as the 'mid-life crisis'. However I still had only my personal experience on which to draw, but as the lecture progressed, and was followed by questions, it became abundantly clear that this fairly sophisticated audience was highly involved. I had struck a note or perhaps more precisely a chord of recognition. My personal experiences were, I now . felt, accurately mirroring a widely experienced phase of life. A few more lectures followed and I became increasingly excited and absorbed by the topic. People were readily identifying with what I was saying, which was both professionally exciting and personally a relief. A journalist with whom I had collaborated on many articles for magazines and a newspaper contacted me, and we agreed to do an article on what I now confidently called the mid-life crisis. The only request I made of the journalist, with which she kindly agreed, since it was very much an afterthought on my part, was to place a small notice at the end of the article. This simply stated that I would be interested in hearing from those men who felt the article reflected some of their experiences.

The response was surprising in that I received over 100 letters, all expressing their writers' sense of identification with the article. The mail was sufficiently prolific to become the source of some good-humoured envy amongst colleagues, who referred to it as 'fan-mail'. With stunning regularity, letter after letter expressed a smiliar pattern of recognition of the feelings and difficulties discussed in the article.

Such statements as 'I am forty years of age, married seventeen years with four children. Most of my life I have been the "achiever" type and suffered from "over-driving" myself and low esteem', dominated the letters. One man captured the difficulty of dealing with the feelings experienced during this period: 'It seems that whenever it is mentioned the usual reply from the family doctor, the wife, the boss etc. is "don't worry" or "why don't you have a long holiday without the kids?" or "why not change your job?" ' — responses so glib as to betray a complete lack of knowledge of the area and problems.

Another writer indicated a ready recognition of symptoms:

> I am 39 years of age, a real estate manager and the stress symptoms, irritability, fatigue, depression and general dissatisfaction fit me to a 'T'.

The same man ventured this insight:

> It is strange, that basically I seek success primarily to improve my family's lot — yet in seeking that success I am quite likely to lose them altogether.

A letter from a young, highly successful, self-employed businessman, 31 years of age, captures much of the general theme of the letters:

> It may sound funny but my wife and I are happily married but I feel my life is finished . . . surely all that I have achieved and done, that isn't the end is it? I worry about what else I can do in life.

Two very successful businessmen in their early 40s offered these succinct reflections. One said:

> My problem is less one of marriage problems and work pressures, than in defining what I want to do with the rest of my life, based on the thinking that *there has to be a better way*.

The other, having spent an earlier period of three years actually doing what must be a universal fantasy for mid-life crisis males, that is, sailing around the world, had now returned and had this view:

> I find myself back in the same old routine, same old rat-race, competing with the Joneses and being tied

hand and foot running the company I formed 18 years ago — There just must be a better way.

Finally, a formerly self-employed professional man of 52 years had this to say:

I have given my life to many people and had to be there, locked into a system that required me, hail, rain or shine, sick or well. I want to give more of my life to me, I value me.

He had chosen to withdraw from an active business life to lead a simple uncluttered one, and now saw his situation in terms of seeking 'not approval from anyone, just joy, pleasure, human warmth and affection'.

I found it very moving to read these letters, and to have men share, in writing, their inner fears and insecurities. These were letters from men in a culture that reinforces the tough, all-male, masculine traits and denigrates any obvious displays of feeling or sentiment. There was now ample evidence that from my initial very personal doubts I had moved to a clear recognition of a phenomenon of considerable substance. What did surprise me was how consistently a man's occupation denied him, or deprived him of, the opportunity for fulfilment. Almost without exception, the men who wrote to me were successful by ordinary standards, sometimes highly successful, but plagued, like I was, with a sense of purposelessness and futility.

I vividly remember the sense of excitement that accompanied my reading the letters, along with the feeling of relief. Relief on two fronts: one, that I was not alone and secondly, that despite the environment in which I was working, where rational thought constituted a god, I had listened to my inner promptings and perhaps inadvertently unearthed one of the clues for dealing with the crisis — trust your inner voice, or alternatively, back your hunch!

The odd aspect of all this was that at no time had I set out a plan: I had rather stumbled, fell, or leaped from one moment of time to the next. Here I was now with an enormous pile of letters, letters that were replete with intimate thoughts and expressions of despair, anxiety, depression and disillusionment. After a period of uncertainty I decided to reply to as many letters as I could, inviting the writer to contact me with a view to making a mutually convenient time for discussion. At this point the undertaking, starting from a very personal beginning, was taking on the form of a piece of psychological research. My academic conditioning, euphemistically described as education, warned — no, rather screamed at — me that one could not undertake research until the research design had been clearly formulated. This involved such issues as the nature of the sample and the methods used, which relate to such tasks as deciding who I would interview and how I would obtain the subjects, what would be the content and format of data collection and so on. In an academic framework I anticipated that my peers would want to know the means I used to analyze the so-called data and my justification for the choice. I knew that if I were doing 'proper research' I would think through all these issues and endow the findings with legitimacy by producing a tight, quantitative statistical analysis of the data. Then I could assert with the certainty of a 'real' scientist that my findings were significant beyond the .001 level of chance. In doing so I would have experienced the security of the factual male world and removed myself from the threat of inner chaos and uncertainty that pervaded my being, as it did those of the men who had trusted me sufficiently to write. Here I was experiencing the very type of pressure that I was trying to work my way through, the pressure to be rational and competent, not confused, irrational and unclear.

A touch of irony at this time was that as part of my lecturing duties I was responsible for teaching research methods, and here was I violating every known rule. Once again I felt out of step with the outside world and yet driven and pushed from the inside to struggle with the questions and issues of which I had now become aware. Was I to concede and begin to formulate my questions with clarity, or was I to stumble on? In a sense there was no choice, since my uneasiness about seeing the world in tight, empirical, rigid and academic terms was reaching acute proportions.

Such questions as 'What do I want to prove?' found no ready, acceptable answer, and further, I felt disinclined to follow the rules, since it was in partially breaking free of them that I had been able to arrive at, and recognize, this

9

particular human phenomenon.

Finally the issues dissolved when I decided that I would simply talk with each of the men who responded to my invitation to do so. My only aim at this stage was to see if they could share with me some of their feelings and thoughts about this particular stage in their lives. Approximately 40 men responded and we talked from a minimum of one hour to as long as three hours in a free, flowing, unstructured interchange. Each conversation had the peculiar quality of being unique and yet the same. Through them I was given what I have come to regard as a superb and privileged opportunity to experience the sharing of uncertainties. My life has been indelibly altered and enriched by these meetings, during which I was constantly struck by the intensity of the men's feelings and the disarming honesty with which they shared them. The sessions remain firmly in my memory as moments during which human frailty and vulnerability — rather than a brittle facade of all-embracing competence — were the cornerstone. It is the knowledge that I gleaned from these conversations that I share in this book.

Indeed it was only after some 15-20 interviews that I began to think that perhaps I could produce a book which, apart from assisting me with my mid-life crisis, might also assist other men to locate their own pain and confusion within a framework that rendered it more accessible and less threatening. I had experienced the benefit of knowing myself not to be the only 'misfit'; the men I spoke with expressed the healing quality of this knowledge: it seemed possible that others could benefit if I could capture the crisis on paper, in book form.

From this point on, when I actually started to try and write, I was besieged by periods of grave self-doubt as to whether I could capture the essence of those conversations. I found myself, and still find myself as I now write, falling back on the well-imprinted academic patterns that form part of the logical, rational, factual male world. This produces a sense of panic, and flight to seek and ascertain the prevailing expert opinion. I have lost count of the number of times I have felt compelled to look up references, seek evidence, know the facts before I start, etc. In short, I have felt crippled by these thoughts and rendered impotent in the task of putting pen to paper. It is my past successes as an academic that now haunt me, and threaten the pursuit of my inner promptings. So many of the men expressed this sort of struggle; often, so very often, they intuitively knew what they wanted, but past patterns offered security and the guarantee of acceptance — their refusal to overthrow these patterns prevented any resolution of the crisis.

Gradually, however, as I listened to the men talking again (since, with their permission, I had tape-recorded all the interviews), the potency and richness of these conversations restored my confidence: I felt able to tackle the task once again, and did so in such a manner that their stories formed the essence of the book. Hence this book is not a textbook, and it is limited in the number of references and amount of substantiating material, and all that normally constitutes proof or evidence. To have attempted to fulfil these requirements, like those of the research requirements, seemed like an inappropriate step for me and a violation of the spirit of the interviews themselves.

This is not to say that there has not been valid and useful material written on the topic, although, in the main, it is very scarce. But as part of preparing this book, when driven by my rational-empirical self, I did ascertain two excellent sources: *Passages* by Gail Sheehy, and *Seasons of a Man's Life* by Levinson *et al.* However, both of these books deal with the mid-life crisis within the broader context of the whole family life cycle. For me, it was the specific stage of mid-life that was absorbing and in this context the two major sources of stimulus, reinforcement and courage were the writings of Carl Gustav Jung and the poetry of T.S. Eliot.

The former provided the necessary theoretical link and framework for my experiences, the latter confirmed the spirit of the experiences. Jung's work is wide ranging, complex and esoteric; however a central theme is his notion — Jung would probably declare it an empirical fact — of the *anima*, the soul or spirit in man. It is the inevitable inner demand for expression by this aspect of the male psyche that I am now convinced is central to the mid-life crisis. Other writers,

11

while discussing the mid-life crisis, barely mention, if at all, this vital idea. As my interviews progressed with the men it became very clear to me that a wider discussion of the anima concept could prove of considerable value to males in the mid-life crisis. Much of this present book owes an intellectual debt to the genius and wisdom of Jung.

The crisis can be seen in the specific context of a male mid-life crisis, or alternatively, in the wider context of internal/external conflict: the constant challenge to follow one's inner promptings often in the face of a contradictory and polarized external reality. Thus what I have written simply represents one form, one language, of what can be regarded as the universal conversation between the opposites within ourselves as we move slowly, but inevitably, towards integration. Much of the anxiety that the men I interviewed experienced emanated from their inability to recognize that these opposites are continually dancing within, and that outer conflicts are often simply the externalization of the inner play. However, until we recognize that outside is inside and inside is outside then we will go on drawing artificial boundaries that exclude the possibility of resolution. When we are able to glimpse that our discontent about such outside matters as our occupation or status is in fact a manifestation of a deeper and profound struggle within, then resolution emerges as at least a possibility. Yet everyday living encourages ·externalization, as people seek frantically for solutions outside themselves in the form of possessions, attachments, etc. etc. Most of the men I shared time with had reached a point in their lives where they realized that there did not exist any external solutions: 'they had met the enemy and it was them'! To continue to seek external solutions to intrinsically internal dilemmas struck most of them as an act of self-deception. Yet little existed in the way of guidelines for internal solutions. Whilst this author is not capable of or committed to the idea of providing solutions, this book will perhaps serve to map a part of the journey, and in so doing, to reveal that others have been there before.

1 Others have been there before!

In the middle of the journey of our life, I came to myself within a dark wood where the straight way was lost. Ah, how hard it is to tell of that wood, savage and harsh and dense, the thought of which renews my fear. So bitter is it death is hardly more.

Dante wrote these words in the 14th century when he was 42. They are the opening stanzas of *The Divine Comedy*. A literary figure of equal stature, John Milton, wrote the folllowing lines:

Which way shall I fly
Infinite wrath and infinite despair?
Which way I fly is hell; myself am hell;
And in the lowest deep a lower deep,
Still threat'ning to devour me, opens wide.
To which the hell I suffer seems a heaven.

Dante's masterpiece was begun at the age of 37 following his banishment from Florence where, two years previously, as an idealist and with the 'proper' trappings of life, he had been elected one of the chief magistrates of Florence. But in 1302, he was convicted of refusing to recognize the Pope's authority in civil matters. This conviction resulted in him being dispossessed and banished from Florence. Hence Dante's words, like Milton's, can be seen as powerful statements of profound psychological depth, depicting the opening scene, for which much of the script had already been experienced, of the mid-life journey. The pervasive and dominant themes are those of loss, confusion, despair and fear.

Seemingly far removed from both Dante and Milton is the 19th century Russian playwright, Anton Tchekov. But not removed in time or spirit is the main character, Ivan, in Tchekov's play *Ivanov*. Here is Ivan calling off his wedding to Sasha:

> I've worn myself out. At thirty-five I feel like a man after a drunken bout, I'm old already. I've put on an old man's dressing-gown. I go about with a heavy head, with a lazy soul, tired and broken, without faith, without love, without aim; I wander about among my friends like a shadow and I don't know who I am, or why I live, or what I want. Already it seems to me that love is silly, that caresses and endearments are sugary nonsense, that there isn't any meaning in work, that song and impassioned words are trivial and old fashioned. And wherever I go I bring misery, blank boredom, discontent, disgust with life . . . I'm ruined, hopelessly ruined! Before you stands a man tired at thirty-five, disenchanted, crushed by his trivial efforts — burning with shame and jeering at his own weakness . . . Oh, how my pride revolts.

Despite desperate pleas from Sasha, Ivan finally commits suicide and thus leaves the reader in little doubt as to the intensity of this period in his life. Tchekov, himself, was 27 when he wrote these lines, lines which capture the full range and potency of the feelings that can erupt for men at this time in their lives. Although suicide may not be the preferred solution for most sufferers, it became clear to me, both from my own life and from the lives of many of the men I talked with, that the thought of destroying oneself, as a final explicit statement on the sense of futility, was very common. Eliot Jaques, an English psychoanalyst and one of the few scholars who has been concerned with the mid-life crisis, focussed on the issue of death and its relationship to the crisis. In a random sample of some 310 famous painters, composers, poets, writers and sculptors, he found a dramatic

14

and sudden jump in the death rate between 35 and 39, during which time it was far in excess of the norm or average. Within his sample he included such outstanding creative personalities as Mozart, Raphael, Chopin, Purcell and Baudelaire.

Whilst there may be a variety of reasons for the deaths of these artists around the age of 37, it is nonetheless interesting that they should have occurred at this particular stage of life, a time when, for many individuals, a profound psychological journey is underway. Other artists can be seen to have reacted in different ways to the same inner sense of writhing discontent. Gauguin is perhaps the case *par excellence* of the mid-life crisis: in his early to middle thirties he gave up his bank career, left his wife, and, by the age of 41, had become a leading Post-Impressionist painter. Albert Schweitzer is another classic example: at the age of 30 he forsook a brilliant university and musical career to study medicine in order to become a missionary doctor. At the age of 38 he renounced fame and fortune as an exponent of J.S. Bach and departed for Lambaréné in French Equatorial Africa to set up his mission hospital.

There may be a tendency for some readers — hoping to protect themselves from the pain and chaos of this middle period in their lives — to dismiss the preceding material as simply being about famous people and having nothing to do with themselves.

This would be a mistake since writers, painters and other highly creative people are different only in their capacity to capture and give expression to what is fundamental and intrinsic to us all. In this context T.S. Eliot displays an extraordinary ability to give form to a man's inner struggles — take these lines from *East Coker*:

So here I am, in the middle way, having had twenty years —
Twenty years largely wasted, the years of *l'entre deux guerres* —
Trying to learn to use words, and every attempt
Is a wholly new start, and a different kind of failure.

These lines can be interpreted as Eliot's own struggle with his sense of personal inadequacy — a struggle that explodes into consciousness for many men in the decade between

15

35 and 45 years. An even more precise statement by Eliot, written when he was 47, and perhaps reflective of the turmoil experienced at such a time, is to be found in *The Dry Salvages*:

> Trying to unweave, unwind, unravel
> and piece together the past and the future,
> Between midnight and dawn, when the past is all deception,
> The future futureless, before the morning watch
> When time stops and time is never ending

Here Eliot gives poetic form to the unceasing task and the uncertainty that plagues men and devours their confidence as the past becomes of negligible use in facing and understanding the present moment.

Interwoven throughout much of Eliot's poetry is his brilliant and highly creative perception and awareness of time. For many men time becomes a reality, a painful reality, in their late thirties or early forties. They become aware that it is finite for them and hence simultaneously often catch a first glimpse of their own inevitable mortality. As will be discussed in greater detail later, death, particularly the death of a close friend or relative, brings into consciousness the finiteness of time and the initial awareness that many hopes, dreams, wishes and aspirations are not going to be fulfilled. Eliot says it eloquently and forcibly in *Burnt Norton*:

> If all time is eternally present
> All time is unredeemable
> What might have been is an abstraction
> Remaining a perpetual possibility
> Only in a world of speculation.

The inevitable heightened awareness of time can be used for many purposes. Among these are self-recrimination, leading to depression; a desperate clinging to what was, leading to fear; perpetual nostalgia, a desperate attempt to turn time back and recapture one's elusive youth, leading to jealousy and resentment. On the other hand this awareness may provide an opportunity to reflect on the challenge to growth inherent in the second half of life.

Jung expresses his view succinctly when he says:

Middle life is the moment of greatest unfolding, when a man still gives himself to his work with his whole strength and his whole will. But in this very moment evening is born, and the second half of life begins. Passion now changes her face and is called duty; I want becomes the inexorable I must and the turnings of the pathway that once brought surprise and discovery become dulled by custom. The wine has fermented and begins to settle and clear. Conservative tendencies develop if all goes well; instead of looking forward one looks backward, most of the time involuntarily, and one begins to take stock, to see how one's life has developed up to this point. The real motivations are sought and real discoveries are made. The critical survey of himself and his fate enables a man to recognise his peculiarities. But these insights do not come to him easily; they are gained only through the severest shocks.

The conversations I had with men in this phase of their lives leaves little doubt as to the 'severest shocks'. However, of equal certainty was that we as a society are retarded and limited in our ability to cultivate, encourage, or simply render permissible the reflective attitude necessary if a man is to develop a pathway toward resolution of this dilemma. Rather it is activity and flight into the outside world, the maniacal construction of materialistic distractions, that characterize the acceptable solutions in our affluent 20th century western world. Reflection has somehow got confused with sloth or old age and the very process that facilitates the possibility of meeting this creative challenge in life, is lost. This, above all else, is what struck me about the men's lives — they were lost in a world of materialism that had lost its capacity to sustain their being, they were T.S. Eliot's 'hollow men':

We are the hollow men
We are the stuffed men
Leaning together
Headpiece filled with straw. Alas!
Our dried voices, when
We whisper together

Are quiet and meaningless
As wind in dry grass
Or rats' feet over broken glass
In our dry cellar

When we sever the pathway between the conscious mind and our unconscious, then it is little wonder that 'Our dried voices, when we whisper together are quiet and meaningless', as the rats' feet scramble over the broken glass of our lost and shattered fantasies and dreams. As will become apparent, this theme (with particular stress being laid on a specific aspect of the unconscious mind, the *anima* in Jungian terms), is central to this book. As Emma Jung so clearly states:

The anima represents the connection with the spring or source of life in the unconscious.

Without this spring, the 'hollow men' and their dryness will be the fate of many men. Frantic and desperate pursuits of external distractions or external rewards such as affluence, power and status can only, as my conversations elucidated, lead to a nagging sense of hollowness. Yet the paradox, as will emerge, is that any alternative pursuits are difficult to sustain, since to choose an individual path must always result in a violation of the group's beliefs and, consequently, hostility towards the wayward member.

If there is a positive, growth-producing potential in the mid-life crisis, if there is an alternative to the 'hollow men' and if during this period discoveries are to be made as Jung suggests, then how can these things be realized, what form do these processes take? Without anticipating too much of the discussion to follow it seems appropriate to at least explore, in a preliminary matter, this other face of the mid-life crisis, and to do so through three outstanding figures. This time I have restricted my focus to three giants in the field I know best, psychology. They are Gustav Fechner, Sigmund Freud and Carl Gustav Jung.

Marie-Louise von Franz, in quoting Jung, provides a clear statement of the task in middle life when she says:

While in the first half of life consciousness grows out of a purely natural basis provided by the instincts and strives primarily for the goal of social adaptation and achievement, a fundamental change takes place in middle life — it is as if the sun, after crossing the meridian, drew in its rays, in order to illumine itself, after having squandered its light on the world.

It is the 'in order to illumine itself' analogy which is the apposite point, since the mid-life position is the serious beginning to this task. Jung himself, in discussing the mid-life period, makes the following observation:

For a young person it is almost a sin . . . to be too pre-occupied with himself; but for the ageing person it is a duty and a necessity to devote serious attention to himself.

The term 'ageing person' can be taken here to mean anyone of 35 years plus, since at this point we are truly midway through our lives and ageing is the valid description, albeit perhaps an unacceptable one! However, this 'in order to illumine itself' process is a difficult journey likely to contain severe shocks. Indeed, a process described by some authors as a 'creative illness' appears — given the documented age at onset, the symptoms and duration — to be similar to, if not identical with, the mid-life crisis. Henri Ellenberger, in his mammoth work entitled *The Discovery of the Unconscious*, puts forward the idea that the development of dynamic psychiatry owes much of its origin to the so-called 'creative illness' of Freud and Jung respectively. He lists the main symptoms of creative illness as depression, exhaustion, irritability, sleeplessness and headaches. The person going through such an illness, according to Ellenberger, 'lives in spiritual isolation and has the feeling that nobody can help him, hence his attempts at self-healing'. This feeling was consistently present among the men I interviewed; indeed, most believed that no-one could understand their dilemma. This feeling led to a further increase in their sense of alienation and made them even less accessible to help of any form. Almost invariably did they express amazement at the relevance of the newspaper article that they had responded to. This clearly indicates not the brilliance of the article, but the negative and pernicious effects of the isolation that seems to inevitably accompany the mid-life crisis. Perhaps the first step in devoting 'serious attention to himself' is for a man to undergo some form of withdrawal. Eliot Jaques's

19

views are consistent with this point: he sees the crisis as essentially a period when 'unconscious depressive anxieties are aroused', as 'essentially a period of purgatory — anguish and depression'. Each of these feelings is likely to reinforce a man's sense of spiritual isolation and heighten the feeling that nobody can help him.

If one accepts the view that the crisis, adequately worked through, can lead to growth and a deepening of self-understanding, then an interesting connection presents itself: a connection which points toward the possibility of the mid-life crisis being the necessary preliminary to psychological growth and maturation, without which stagnation is the inevitable consequence. Erik Erikson sees this stage of life as being precisely about the issue of stagnation versus generativity. Generativity means finding ways to accept one's own authority, which in the main is derived from the painful process of having come to an understanding of one's own vulnerabilities as well as strengths. The mid-life crisis perhaps only becomes a 'creative' illness when this awareness is integrated with an appreciation of one's strengths and a clearer perception of purpose. This last point of renewed purpose is a vital sign of successful resolution. Put another way, a restructuring of one's vision that is consistent with substantial increase in self-knowledge, seems to characterize the outcome of a creative illness. This is most certainly so in the case of Fechner, Freud and Jung as we shall now see. They provide examples *par excellence* of how to convert the mid-life crisis into a 'creative illness'.

Gustav Fechner is best known as the pioneer of experimental psychology, which found its starting point in two volumes — entitled *Elements of Psycho-Physics* — which he published in 1860. What is perhaps less well known is the extent to which Freud, in his pioneering work, drew on Fechner's ideas. However for the present purpose, the more important information concerns his creative illness. In 1833 at the age of 32, Fechner married and took up the post of Professor of Physics at Leipzig University. It is reported that from 1834 to 1840 Fechner pursued this occupation under considerable strain and finally, at the age of 39, collapsed and had to give up his professional activities for three years.

During this time, according to Walter Lowrie:

> Fechner felt compelled to live in complete seclusion, remaining in a darkened room, the walls of which were painted black or wearing a mask on his face so as to shut out the light. He was unable to tolerate most foods, felt no hunger and ate very little so that his physical condition became precarious.

His care constitutes another story concerning a lady friend who dreamed of cooking a certain meal for him, which she actually did and also insisted that he ate it, resulting in his cure. However, the three-year depression — which can be seen as an acute mid-life crisis — culminated in his conviction that he had discovered a universal principle that was as important and basic to the spiritual world as Newton's principle of gravitation to the physical world: this he called *das Lustprinzip* (the principle of pleasure). Whether Fechner's 'unversal principle' is true or not is beside the point. What is important to note is, firstly, that Fechner is reported to have lived in perfect health for the remainder of his life, finally dying of old age at 86; secondly, and germane to this idea of a creative illness resulting in a renewed purpose, is the fact that although prior to his illness he had been a physicist and reputedly very antagonistic toward philosophy, after the illness he exchanged his professorship of physics for that of philosophy and thereafter never ceased developing his idea of the principle of pleasure. It is obvious from such a transition of interests that Fechner had undergone a period of considerable change or metamorphosis during his mid-life crisis which set him on a different path, seemingly more consistent with his personality and needs than that of the first half of his life. Evidence for the consistency of this second path can be gleaned from the fact that, despite his apparent antagonism toward natural philosophy, Fechner had previously published several literary pamphlets under a pseudonym and in 1836 he published a book on the stages of human life entitled *The Little Book of Life after Death*. This he did whilst holding the hard-nosed scientific position of professor of physics. But the singularly important point to note is the painful, disturbing and depressing period of three years that elapsed prior to the

21

resolution. It is also clear that the apparently sudden collapse had in fact been building for some five years, years which, by external standards, were extremely successful, commencing with his appointment to a professorial position at the age of 32.

Amongst the men I interviewed, the phenomenon of a 'collapse' as such was not uncommon. One man who was in his mid-thirties at the time of interviewing described how, after having achieved a high-level managerial position in a large manufacturing firm, he had found himself one night, 'After everyone had gone sitting alone in my office and I completely broke down, crying, sobbing, uncontrollably . . . I never went back again after that day'. To him, such behaviour was completely out of character and inexplicable, although in retrospect he could see that the feelings had been slowly building over a three-year period; also he had observed in himself an increasing tendency to avoid making decisions of any kind. This is from a senior management executive who reached the top ranks at 30, and had all the trappings of success — company car, overseas trips, etc. He, like Fechner, had a prolonged period of non-communication and a severe loss of confidence to the extent that he could not even answer a telephone. Although he received anti-depressant medication, he only took the medication for a short period and finally, consistent with the idea of a creative illness, took to making small wooden objects, after which he carried out considerable renovations on his house, both inside and outside. He had not, prior to his illness, had any inclination or ability to work with his hands, but the illness had brought to the fore a method for self-healing which, symbolically, can be seen as self-renovation, externally manifested in his house renovations. He claimed that under-taking these tasks was not planned or thought out in advance, it simply occurred to him spontaneously. Equally can one see this as the mechanism of self-healing operating, consistent with Ellenberger's idea of the 'creative illness'. No doubt the solution will be different for each man — as was markedly the case with Fechner and this man — but what seems critical is that a solution be consistent with the emerging self that has undergone the 'period of purgatory — of anguish and depression', to use Jaques's phrase.

This consistency is most clearly seen in the situations of Freud and Jung, and it is to Freud's creative illness or mid-life crisis that we now turn. Surrounding Sigmund Freud, the founder of psychoanalysis, is a virtual mountain of factual and legendary material. To present his biography in any detail is far beyond the scope of this book and in fact has been beyond most biographers, perhaps with the single exception of Ernest Jones, whose biography on Freud is close to the 'official' one. What is of immediate interest is a distinct period in Freud's life between the years 1894 and 1899, during which Freud was between 38 and 43 years of age, in short, within the range of a mid-life crisis. At the beginning of 1894 Freud suffered from heart symptoms and consulted his close acquaintance, Wilhelm Fliess, who was, curiously enough, an ear, nose and throat specialist! To Freud, however, he was a trusted confidant, one to whom, throughout this period, Freud appears to have been emotionally attached. This relationship with Fliess is interpreted by Ellenberger as reflecting Freud's need, amidst the feelings of isolation indicative of a creative illness, for a guide, a father-figure. In 1896 Freud's father died. As has already been mentioned, the death of a relative seems to herald the awareness of one's mortality and often signals the commencement of the mid-life crisis. This would certainly seem to be so in Freud's case: Ellenberger reports that for about one year after his father's death Freud's inner conflict increased and he brooded constantly over the question of the origin of neurosis. He had, since the time he spent with Charcot in France, had a craving for the 'great discovery' that would bring him fame. It was in unravelling the origin of neurosis that Freud now sought that fame. Apparently he had periods when he felt on the verge of discovering great secrets but then quickly became besieged with self-doubts. In a letter to Fliess in 1897 he wrote: 'the main patient who keeps me busy is myself'.

During this time Ellenberger suggests that 'intellectual speculation, self-analysis and work with his patients occurred in a kind of desperate search for an elusive truth'. Isolation was a constant companion for Freud during these six years, although there is evidence that this was more imagined than real. His self-analysis was arduous and painful as he explored and analyzed his own childhood in a meticulous manner. Jones, in an admittedly biassed account, claims that Freud's self-analysis was an heroic feat without precedence. At the beginning of 1898 he began writing a book on dreams, which was completed in 1899 under the now-famous title *The Interpretation of Dreams*. This was the resolution and the culmination of a profound inner experience that had far-reaching effects on Sigmund Freud as a person.

To place these brief biographical notes in context, it may be helpful to recapitulate Ellenberger's views of a creative illness. He says:

> A creative illness succeeds a period of intense pre-occupation with an idea and search for a certain truth. It is a polymorphous condition that can take the shape of depression, neurosis, psychosomatic ailments or even psychoses. Whatever the symptoms, they are felt as painful, if not agonizing, by the subject with alternating periods of alleviation and worsening... Throughout the illness the subject never loses the thread of his dominating preoccupation... he is almost entirely absorbed within himself. The subject emerges from his ordeal with a permanent transformation in his personality and the conviction that he has discovered a great truth or a new spiritual world.

Clearly this description is an accurate one of Sigmund Freud during this period of his mid-life transition; it is equally valid as a description of Fechner. Furthermore, the men I interviewed, whilst not being in the genius category of Sigmund Freud, nevertheless exhibited much of the same pattern. Particularly evident were the condition of self-absorption and periods of agonizing self-doubts. What perhaps is the most extraordinary feature of Freud's crisis is the self-healing capacity that grew out of his arduous and exhausting self-analysis. The other critical factor in a creative illness, one that Freud so clearly exhibits, is the sustaining question, the dominating preoccupation with an idea. For many men the sustaining question was simply not formulated; they often had no sense of what to ask or how to shape it, which inevitably led them to remain in the depressive phase and not emerge with resolution and a re-formed vision. I suspect that an attitude of courage, courage to explore the intrinsic personal meaning of the crisis, is the real art in the middle of life. Both Freud and Jung displayed such courage. The exploration can take any number of forms, not necessarily that of self-analysis as Freud pursued. Basic and fundamental to the form however is the quality of it being directed and produced from within. So many of the men I spoke with had inner notions of what they desired to do, very clear inner direction, but they simply lacked the courage and confidence to allow it to form. This lack is not wholly theirs as individuals, it also reflects the lack or even absence of social reinforcement for such a pattern in the broader society. They were driven in the right vehicle, themselves, by the wrong driver, external social demands, and almost without exception found it extremely difficult to change drivers! It is only by reflecting on the lives of such great pioneers as Sigmund Freud that one can appreciate the enormous leap of faith and courage that they exhibited. Jung's succinct statement, 'From the middle of life onward, only he remains vitally alive who is ready to die with life', captures the essential quality of this courage.

Jung himself, the founder of analytical psychology, lived a life which reflected his active commitment to this viewpoint. Carl Gustav Jung was born in Switzerland in 1875, lived his entire life there, and died in Küsnacht on the shores of Lake Zurich in 1961. Although he actively collaborated with Freud from 1906 to 1913, it is erroneous to consider him a follower of the latter. Jung had begun his own explorations into the human psyche quite separately from Freud, and apart from the seven years of collaboration, he continued throughout his life to develop his own unique theory of psychology. Jung's life, as does Freud's, forms a book in its own right and is most comprehensively contained in the work entitled *Memories, Dreams, Reflections of C.G. Jung*. What is of particular interest is a specific period of six years, similar in many respects to Freud's, between the years 1913 and 1919. Beyond coincidence is the fact that Jung, like Freud, was between 38 and 42 years of age during this time, again the time of the mid-life crisis. During the first half of his life, Jung, together with Freud, believed that he could develop a new scientific theory of the psyche. The year 1913 when Jung turned 38 seems to have been a critical year. In a short period he broke with Freud, resigned his professorial post at the University of Zurich, resigned from the Psychoanalytic Association and relinquished the editorship of the professional journal, *Jahrbuch*.

These changes represent potent external symbols of transition. However in December 1913 the inner world made its potent comment with the following dream. Jung writes:

> I was with an unknown, brown-skinned man, a savage, in a lonely rocky mountain landscape. It was before dawn, the eastern sky was already bright, and the stars were fading. Then I heard Siegfried's horn sounding over the mountain and I knew that we had to kill him. We were armed with rifles and lay in wait for him on a narrow path over the rocks.
>
> Then Siegfried appeared high up on the crest of the mountain, in the first ray of the rising sun. On a chariot made of the bones of the dead he drove at furious speed down the precipitous slope. When he turned a corner, we shot at him, and he plunged down, struck dead.
>
> Filled with disgust and remorse for having destroyed something so great and beautiful, I turned to flee; impelled by the fear that the murder might be discovered. But a tremendous downfall of rain began, and I knew that it would wipe out all traces of the dead. I had escaped the danger of discovery; life could go on, but an unbearable feeling of guilt remained.

Jung, when he awoke from this dream, could not understand the manifestation and attempted to fall asleep again. However an inner prompting, or rather an inner command in the form of a voice within him, said, 'You must understand this dream and do so at once', followed by, 'If you do not understand the dream you must shoot yourself'. As Jung had a loaded revolver in his night table, he became frightened and began pondering the dream once again, this time resulting in an increased understanding. In commenting on the dream Jung noted that the legendary Siegfried of German tradition, the hero of Wagner's operas, embodied his own attitude and the attitude of the Germans at the time. Both he, and the Germans, believed in the power of will, and in the heroic imposition of their will. The young savage, on the other hand, he saw as representing primitive man who follows his instincts, and it was this figure who had taken the initiative in killing the hero Siegfried. The rain, according to Jung, announced the resolution of the tension between the conscious and the unconscious aspects of his psyche.

This dream and the accompanying interpretative comments reflect a critical moment in Jung's life, since from this period on he pursued the inner journey of exploration. The 'death of the hero' represents the passing or death of the first half of life. Marie-Louise von Franz, Jung's collaborator for over 25 years, has this to say bout the dream:

> This is a typical dream of middle life. All the goals of social adaptation and achievement have been attained and now the hero, which is the midday sun, must die in order to avoid blocking the way for new life.

Six days before this dream Jung had committed himself, even at the risk of sacrificing his own sanity, to confront and explore the depths of his psyche. In other words, he committed himself to the powerful urge from within to shun power, status, prestige and other manifestations of the hero in order to know himself. His sustaining purpose throughout this period of his life was his conviction that he could not help people with their fantasies and dreams until he knew them from his own direct experience. Jung began by writing down his dreams every morning and, secondly, by telling himself stories and prolonging them by writing down everything that his imagination could dictate.

Gradually Jung emerged from his self-imposed experiment and in so doing he made another notable discovery, to which he gave the name *individuation*. This will be discussed in greater detail later but suffice it to say that the term refers to Jung's recognition that the process he had engaged in led the individual to the discovery of the central core of his being, the *Self*. At the beginning of 1919 Jung terminated his experiment, from which he indubitably emerged as a transformed person.

With respect to the mid-life crisis it is worth repeating that this incredible inner journey that Jung undertook occurred between the ages of 38 and 44. According to Ellenberger's ideas it is clear that Jung, like Freud, experienced a creative illness during the mid-life transition. He, like Freud, underwent self-imposed psychic exercises which in effect constituted self-therapy, the self-healing quality of the creative illness. Like Fechner and Freud, Jung made severe cuts in his connections with the outside world. This self-imposed exile reflects the self-absorption quality of the creative illness. Finally, Jung, like Freud, emerged from this period with a highly developed sense of purpose, a clear vision which sustained him for the remainder of his life: namely, the exploration of the inner world of man's psyche.

What is striking about both Jung and Freud is their self-directed and self-imposed analysis, considered by them a necessary prelude to their offering therapeutic aid to others. An unusual parallel to this phenomenon exists amongst ancient *shamans* or medicine men, where it is called an 'initiatory illness'. Primitive healers, such as the Aboriginal medicine men, acquire status through a long and difficult training usually received from other healers. According to Ackerknecht, the only true shamans are those who become shamans after undergoing a peculiar state of mental illness. This can be clearly seen in the following description of an initiatory illness of a Siberian shaman quoted by Ellenberger:

> Nioradze relates how the young man who has received the calling withdraws from society; he spends his nights on the naked ground or even in the snow, observes long periods of fasting, suffers great hardships and converses with the spirits; he presents the picture of a severely psychotic individual. However contrasting with an ordinary mental illness this one starts with a shamanistic vocation and during the course of his illness, the patient undergoes professional initiation at the hands of other shamans; the illness ends the very moment the training is completed and the patient himself is proclaimed a shaman.

It is possible that both Jung and Freud underwent an

'initiatory illness', knowing that to be effective healers or shamans, they needed to experience their own inner world and understand their own complexes, vulnerabilities, strengths and weaknesses. If the creative illness has a self-healing capacity, as the evidence seems to indicate, then perhaps the mid-life crisis is also an initiatory illness — that is, an initiation into the second half of our adult life, the half that Jung has seen as being predominantly concerned with spiritual questions. Can we use the mid-life crisis as an initiatory illness to facilitate within ourselves, just as Freud and Jung did, a capacity to be our own shaman? If we are to do so, then it is very clear — from the example of the ancient primitive shamans to the 20th century healers — that we must learn to recognize, in the first instance, our inner voice, and secondly, to communicate with it.

One man with whom I had a counselling relationship told me a story concerning the inner voice which, in this case, spoke so truly of him and at the same time, of most men. The story came out halfway through a counselling session, seemingly unrelated to the overt content, but no doubt systematically related to the covert theme. It went as follows. One day he was free-diving in water that was three to four metres deep, attending to some problem or other on the sea-bed floor. In free-diving one has no mechanical breathing apparatus, and he soon began to run short of breath. He decided to go up to the surface for more air. Apparently the customary way of doing this was to sight the sunlight and head for it. This he did with a hefty push, normally sufficient to get him to the surface by his calculations. Alas! No surface; another push, still no surface. In his panic he let out a small amount of air and to his consternation the bubbles appeared to him to be going down, not up, and in the opposite direction to what he perceived as the direction of the sunlight. A critical moment occurred: would he follow the sunlight as every fraction of his rational mind demanded, or would he follow the seemingly absurd direction of the bubbles which were going downwards? He chose the bubbles and reached the surface. Apparently he had got confused while diving and in fact had mistakenly followed a reflection of the sunlight which led him away from the surface and could have resulted in his death.

I relate this story for one simple reason. He was 39, in the midst of a full-blown mid-life crisis; a highly creative and successful man. But what the story, by way of an analogy, was telling him was that he was risking his life by following the external, reflected glory and 'sunlight' of status, power and success. The right and correct direction for him was to follow the signs and messages that came from within, his 'bubbles', even if they should seem irrational at the time. It was a clear statement, an inner voice, which was directing him to listen inwardly, to tackle the second half of life with a different attitude. As Jung said:

> We cannot live the afternoon of life according to the programme of life's morning; for what was great in the morning will be little at evening, and what in the morning was true will at evening have become a lie.

What I learned from many of the men was that they too had to kill the hero of their morning, their Siegfried of the first half of life. For some men it was not a question of killing the hero, since the 'hero' had committed suicide, leaving the individual with an excessive sense of remorse and burden of guilt to carry. These men were depressed and aimless. The hero was almost invariably to do with an inner image of acquiring power, wealth and status. This hero, like the reflected sunlight, has to be dismissed if the inner voice, Jung's savage, is to be heard. Otherwise the hero may well transform into a fool in the 'evening' of one's life, with the inevitable consequence of stagnation. However, just as Jung's dream revealed feelings of 'disgust and remorse for having destroyed something so great and beautiful', so will each individual have a profound sense of remorse and depression as the end of one hero comes about and the dark journey that precedes the arrival or birth of a new hero commences. The nature of this new hero is a critical factor in deciding to what extent creative use is made of the mid-life transition.

2 The social context

So far we have viewed the mid-life transition through the eyes of the poets and seen evidence of it in the lives of three outstanding psychologists. But in many ways it has had the quality of being 'out there', 'in there' or 'in their imagination'. It is now time to articulate more precisely the essential characteristics of this passage or tunnel through the mid-life period.

Almost inevitably the very idea of a male mid-life crisis evokes derision, both from men and women. Among many women this notion can be seen as male attention-seeking behaviour. Implicit and basic to this view is the feeling that 'men have had it easy', and that 'even if they do have a crisis it's nothing less than they deserve'. Such women, on account of their own deeply-felt sense of injustice, often find it difficult to feel compassion for men who are in the midst of their crisis. Compassion is seen as 'yet again pandering to the male ego'. Often women at this stage in their lives have a growing sense of resentment arising from the feeling that they have received little, if any, understanding from their husbands when they were going through the crisis of caring for very young children. This may well be, regrettably, a valid and accurate perception of the situation. It is therefore easy to see why some women find it difficult to appreciate or empathize with the male going through a crisis,

31

since consciously or unconsciously they will often feel that it is both deserved and justified.

Whilst this view is understandable, it is nevertheless an immature one which has served to exclude the perception that we have all, both male and female, been oppressed by the tyranny of archaic role definitions and social structures. The inability or unwillingness to grasp this broader view contributes substantially to the manifest derision directed towards the phenomenon of the male mid-life crisis. With this situation added to the general male difficulty in expressing feelings, is it any wonder that most men admitted considerable reluctance to sharing the crisis with their wives? The common response to any suggestion that they might share it was 'Oh no! She would think I was silly'. Some of this is, no doubt, an expression of the man's own difficulties in sharing feelings *per se*, but an equal proportion of the awkwardness can be attributed to the prevailing and predominant attitude of many wives.

It is ironical that what can broadly be described as the Women's Movement has had the paradoxical effect of both inhibiting and facilitating an awareness of the male mid-life crisis. The movement has brought into the daylight of consciousness, into the public, as opposed to private arena, the nature of oppression that women underwent, and indeed still undergo, simply because they are female. One negative feature of this has been the tendency amongst some women to develop a form of ideological purity, a type of fixed idea, that results in a zealous, evangelical manifestation of an anti-male attitude. This, as already mentioned, legitimizes a narrow view of the world that excludes the possibility of compassion and empathy for the human situation, whether it happens to be male or female. The necessary simplicity that accompanies such ideological purity, whilst offering a structure within which personal anger and hatred can be legitimized, can only be maintained so long as there exists an 'enemy'. The 'enemy' in this situation is, of course, the male of the species, and the more militant faction of the women's movement has tended to produce a reversal of the struggle rather than a resolution. That is, one sexist structure has been replaced by another. It is this reversal that has further contributed to men, particularly in the mid-life crisis, feeling uncertain and threatened. Whilst specific reactions to this threat vary, amongst the more reflective men the threat has provided the necessary impetus for questioning the meaning of masculinity, in particular the male role.

This questioning, arising out of the uncertainty generated by women questioning their role, forms the major positive gain for men from the women's movement. Undoubtedly, however, as a result of this questioning, many men have felt their masculinity to be under severe challenge, and in some instances this can result in sexual impotence as a physical expression of withdrawal (just as frigidity in women can be seen as their withdrawal in the face of uncertainty in their famale role). Such specific reactions, if added to the growing general sense of inadequacy and uncertainty in men at mid-life, can result in a prolonged period of depression. In this context it may be difficult to accept that the sense of uncertainty generated by the women's movement has any positive features at all. There is, indeed, a tendency for some men to blame it all on those 'men-hating women's libbers'. Alternatively they may react by adopting the philosophy that 'attack is the best form of defence', resulting in the proliferation of machismo-like behaviour that attempts once again to turn the tide of social change back and sees all women as 'castrating bitches'.

The positive effects of uncertainty can only be seen and appreciated if men recognize that rigid definition of the male role is just as oppressive as is that of the female role; and further, that one definition is inextricably derived from the other: challenge one and inevitably will the other be challenged. This interrelationship has made it possible for men to catch an initial glimpse of their own oppression. However, one is reminded of the existentialist philosopher Søren Kierkegaard's statement: 'Freedom is possibility and anxiety is the possibility of freedom'.

So although men may catch a glimpse, so to speak, of their own oppression, it would be naive in the extreme not to recognize that this glimpse will be accompanied by some anxiety. This anxiety is likely to be particularly acute in mid-life, since the very necessary developmental task at this stage of life is to question and evaluate the meaning of one's life. Such an assessment must invariably explore the meaning and satisfaction of being male, that is, the male role.

Due largely to the women's movement and its aftermath, men must now face their highly individual life-development task in a period of major social change in the area of sexual roles. Considering this situation, it can hardly be surprising that we are becoming increasingly aware of a phenomenon called 'the mid-life crisis'. This explains why, although it has been around for centuries as we saw in the last chapter, it is only now being fully recognized. This recognition has only been rendered possible because women began to explore the meaninglessness of their socially defined role. This sense of meaninglessness is a recurring theme amongst men in mid-life — the initial answer to the inevitable question 'What is the point of it all?' tended to be 'There is no point'. However until this position of despair and desperation is reached, as it was for women, then a working out of a more compatible role is not possible. That is, to use W.B. Yeat's words from *The Circus Animals' Desertion*:

Now that my ladder's gone

I must lie down where all ladders start

In the foul rag and bone shop of the heart.

In other words it is by going back into one's feelings, discovering and in some instances rediscovering what is important to oneself and allowing this to determine one's sense of being, that a sense of freedom is achieved. For some men, this undertaking is too threatening, hence they resort to a slightly remodelled version of the traditional male role, which avoids the pain of the mid-life crisis, but denies its creative possibilities. However, such an escape into the comfort of a somewhat remodelled traditional role is unlikely to offer a man a satisfactory long-term resolution.

It is to the specific nature of the crisis and its varied contexts that we now turn.

3 The individual context

The first point to clarify about the mid-life crisis is that contrary to a prevailing view, it is not to be confused with what has been termed the 'male menopause'. Two authors, Derek Bowskill and Anthea Linacre, have written a book simply called *The Male Menopause*; whilst such a title has the appeal of simplicity, it is erroneous to confuse menopause with the mid-life crisis. What Bowskill and Linacre are actually describing is the mid-life crisis, although they consistently refer to this as menopause. This is in spite of the fact that many medical experts seriously question whether such an entity as male menopause exists or not: Bowskill and Linacre, whilst on the one hand conscientiously recording this evidence, then proceed to systematically ignore it. However if the male menopause *does* exist, and there is some evidence that it does, the fact is that the age of onset would be around 45 years of age not 35 years, which is the age at which I would argue that the mid-life crisis commences.

In other words, the male menopause, assuming for the moment it does exist as a definable clinical entity, is likely to occur at the end or closing stages of the mid-life crisis. It is very possible that it is only when men begin to experience physical disturbances that they seek medical help, since by its very nature the mid-life crisis is difficult to define with sufficient clarity to seek help. In other words the male menopause, which is an organic disorder, ought not to be confused with the mid-life crisis, which is a psychological disturbance. This is not to say that the mid-life crisis does not bring with it the associated physical disturbances since it surely does, but side-effects ought not to be confused with aetiology. Likewise, it would be foolish to assert that menopause did not produce psychological problems. The essential point is that menopause on the average has its onset around 45-47 years of age and is a physical disorder with psychological implications. Whereas the mid-life crisis occurs in the span of years a decade before, 35-45 years, and is a psychological disorder with physical implications.

However, as is so often the situation, there is an ever-present tendency to resort to physical explanations in our society, and to see the difficulties as 'menopausal' is a further example of this trend. It is almost as if we have to find a material, physical explanation for our inner psychological discomfort and then somehow we magically feel it is manageable, or at the very least someone else will manage it, namely the medical profession. In many ways the male menopause may well indicate an unresolved mid-life crisis and the men expressing this complaint may well be, at another level, expressing a very different complaint. Amongst those men who resort to the safety and comfort of a physical disturbance, there may well be a pervasive pattern of failure to accept the terror of a mid-life crisis with its attendant sense of despair. This is not to say they do not have very real physical symptoms, rather it is to say that they may well tend to habitually deny inner psychological conflict and constantly externalize it through physical symptoms. In this way they manage to avoid responsibility for it and shift the blame elsewhere, a strategy which in itself negates the possibility of a creative solution of the crisis. It is possible that in these men, the 'male menopause' is strictly speaking a delayed symptom of their unresolved mid-life crisis. Dr Bromley, author of *The Psychology of Human Ageing*, says:

> The existence of the so-called 'male climacteric' is doubtful although the notion had been invoked as an explanation for marked changes in the mid-life behaviour of some men.

Hence attempts to see the mid-life crisis and male menopause as the same phenomenon, whilst having the appeal of an escape, can be shown to be erroneous. They are rather two separate phenomena which may well overlap on occasions, but which, on average, will be approximately ten years apart in age of onset.

If the mid-life crisis is not physical and is not the dreaded 'male menopause', then what is it? As has already been indicated it is a period in a man's life, approximately between the ages of 35 and 45, during which he finds himself caught in an inevitable review of his situation. It is a time of self-assessment when a sufficient period of time as an adult in the workday world has elapsed for one to see how well earlier hopes, fantasies and dreams have been achieved. For some men it is a very nervous blink, for others it is a prolonged, painful, seemingly never-ending stare. It is called the mid-life crisis since in pure statistical terms, given the average age of death around 70, 35 is the true middle of one's life, not 45. The fact that we think of 45 as middle-age is reflective of an illusion that we are all going to live to 90! It is also indicative of one of the major difficulties encountered in the mid-life transition, that of facing the reality of one's mortality. For many men it is around 35 that they first realize in an emotional sense that they are actually going to die. As one man said, 'I finally realized that I was not immortal'. This coincides with an ever-increasing sense and awareness of the ageing process itself. Men become aware of their increasing baldness, their flabby and deteriorating physique and the major discrepancy between the mirror reflection — despite the deep breath to hold one's stomach in — and their memory of the much younger, virile athlete. They often begin to experience their failing physical capacities as they run to the train, in the game of squash, or in the perennial sports match against the students.

All these external physical events provide a stark and often undeniable reminder of age, the coming of age and the passing of youth. This, in a society that idolizes youth and associates it with all the good things in life, is hard to accept and the tendency is to deny the ageing process. Thus suburban streets and local parks are full of desperate, panting joggers attempting to jog age into oblivion and grasp the elixir of youth. It is not the jogging *per se* that is wrong, although one can think of strong arguments against it; it is rather that it is an inappropriate solution to the real dilemma. To try and solve psychological problems physically only seems to achieve a temporary delay of the psychological problems, a temporary reprieve. But it is consistent, in a predominantly materialistic world, a world obsessed with action, that many men's first response to the mid-life crisis should be to resort to a violent outburst of physical exercise. Many men continue to try and resolve the crisis at this level, indulging in even more exercise and deeper suntans, as they desperately reassure themselves that Peter Pan is alive and well.

It became increasingly clear to me throughout the interviews that very early in a man's life a habit of coping with the inner-world phenomenon is established. In general, this is the traditional male habit of externalizing it into the physical world, and as a consequence men often do not seem to develop the mechanism for an attitude of inward reflection. It is as if they have a mirror which only points outward, to the outside world, and that part of the mirror which might reflect inner images is blacked out. Thus men often experience the mid-life crisis as a physical crisis, accompanied by a growing resentment and jealousy of youth. Their intimate personal lives are often characterized by an insensitivity to feelings, an inability to communicate feelings and a taboo against tenderness. These characteristics generally seem to apply to the highly successful all-male beings, whose wives, after 12-15 years of marriage, begin to despair of the possibility of ever achieving any workable level of intimacy with their husbands. Such men are constantly and literally outside themselves, and their preoccupation with the physical dimension is simply a clear manifestation of a much broader 'outsideness'. They find plenty of faults and problems 'outside' themselves — it is either a man's wife, children, friends or his boss who are to blame — but never inside, since the back of the mirror is blacked out. Such men find the mid-life crisis a painful and losing battle, since they lack the essential equipment for resolution: that is, an attitude of inward reflection and a belief that events and phenomena in the outside world are only half the picture. The mid-life crisis for these outer-directed men constitutes a 'crisis of youth' and a fighting battle to ward off the inevitable and biologically-determined process of age. Thus one essential task of the mid-life crisis is to come to an understanding and acceptance of one's age, and to make a readjustment with respect to the future tasks. This does not mean that one sits in a rocking chair at 35 and says 'Now I am an old man'. Rather does it mean a questioning of the appropriate goals for the next period of life, a review of the existing goals, and a moment when one stops, thinks, listens, and waits!

It is this task which, in a world that reinforces action, is difficult to sustain. The inclination is to tackle the problem before it gets on top of one. Or alternatively, to create enough movement and action in one's life to maintain continual distraction. But such action is often motivated by fear, a fear of stopping and finding out that it is all pointless. Many men experience this deep doubt but in the absence of guidelines and established ways of dealing with it, feel that action is the only strategy. In the type of men we have discussed, who are functioning solely on the physical plane, this action tends to be directed to re-establishing potency and power. When this goal coincides with a waning sense of sexual potency then extra-marital liaisons often seem to be the norm — not relationships that lead to a deepening awareness of the possibilities of intimacy, but relationships that, like jogging, are a form of sexual athletics aimed at convincing the male involved of his ongoing potency and existence as a person. This type of reaction is quite understandable for a person whose sense of identity derives from physical prowess: for, to such a one, the fading physical strengths in the mid-life transition can only be experienced as a fading sense of self. This is a frightening prospect and it is little wonder that the sense of one's person ceasing to exist compels many men into seemingly irrational behaviour. Such behaviour may include the impulsive purchasing of grossly inappropriate flashy clothes, drinking bouts, extravagant and flamboyant entertainment, preoccupation with erotica and sexual material of all kinds, and above all else, an obsession with one's physical appearance that is far in excess of any teenager's. In short, such men, whose mid-life crisis is predominantly acted out in the physical mode, are often described as going through a second adolescence. This, as we will discover shortly, is an accurate description.

Another aspect of the physical dimension in the mid-life transition, an aspect that often coexists with the physical exercise pattern, is the acquisition of material possessions. This activity still reflects the externalized search for potency and power and quite often takes on an almost obsessional quality. Behind it is the belief that money and possessions are the source of one's identity. As a result a pattern of acquisition of possessions which are seen as valuable, becomes the primary behaviour. Thus the 'hero' pursued in this pattern is often a cultural stereotype of success, a recognized status symbol. One man whom I interviewed, aged 37, had set himself the goal of buying an expensive motor car, a make which left no doubt as to its owner's status. From his mid-20s he had worked excessively hard, a true self-made businessman, and was now conducting a most successful contracting business. He paid cash for his expensive car, only to find that this purchase was followed by a period of considerable depression and confusion. He had achieved what he defined as the ultimate success in the materialistic world; the question for him now was 'What else?' This was a question to which he had no answer, since his values were tied to the physical and materialistic world, to the values of an affluent society, that sets goals for individuals to pursue; however, having attained these goals, an individual often finds himself left in a state of *ennui*.

The actual achieving of one's dream can be followed by a profound sense of disillusionment, since within himself the man still feels the same sense of wretchedness that is so characteristic of the mid-life crisis. The review and re-evaluation can often take on a more painful form if a man has acquired all the symbols of success — large house, expensive car, large expense account, overseas trips and so forth — and still feels within himself a devastating sense of hollowness. It is far more difficult to make sense of or be open to the inner world when one has been exclusively preoccupied with the outside world, the social world, the ego world, for the first half of one's life. Yet the truth of the matter is that most men *are* in the outside world in the first half of their lives. The salvation for some men is that they never quite believe in it fully and maintain a question with respect to materialism. Somehow they recognize, despite their behaviour to the contrary, that the relentless pursuit of possessions is a cul-de-sac, and that *who* one is, must derive its meaning from a deeper inner source. The mid-life transition, although no less painful for these men, is potentially a more creative opportunity.

One of the distinguishing features of these men is that they seem to have had a more positive relationship with their mothers than those men who pursued materialism unquestioningly. The latter group more frequently expressed admiration for their fathers, particularly their business skills. This is reflected in the unrelenting materialism of the exclusively physically-orientated men leading lives which did not question traditional male values of power, strength, logic and worldly success. Hence the emergence of a sense of disquiet, intrinsic to the mid-life transition, made absolutely no sense to them. The danger is that such men react to the anxiety as a threat and continue their pursuit of possessions and power, only this time round with even more devotion.

The group more closely allied with their mothers almost felt a sense of relief on becoming aware of a mid-life disquiet, the sort of relief that is derived from recognizing something familiar, even if disagreeable. These men had, through their relationship with their mothers, acquired at least the nucleus of an alternative set of values, those of relatedness, nurture and of the legitimacy of feeling. However these values rarely seemed to have survived other than as a vague sort of memory, which was reawakened by the challenge of the mid-life crisis. Often this reawakening brought with it a sense of depression as they reflected on what they now felt to be the futility of the life style they had been living. But in this recognition, in this tension, lies the seeds of a creative solution if the confidence to listen, inwardly, is sufficiently well developed and supported. Otherwise a profound sense of powerlessness, accompanied by withdrawal, both emotional (withdrawal from relationships) and physical (reflected in sexual impotence), tended to be the pattern of response. If a man, for whatever reasons, is unable to evolve a set of meanings and values that apply beyond the physical, material realm, is unable to meet the inner challenge, then it seems likely that the mid-life crisis will be no more than an uncomfortable, irritating period in his life. As Frances Wickes so succinctly states:

> If one chooses refusal of this inner urge, the second half of life is devoted to being a bigger and better caterpillar, or a large dead caterpillar.

Perhaps this failure to rework the dream, to restructure the goals and values, will restate itself in the form that W.B. Yeats describes to us in these lines from the poem entitled *Lines Written in Dejection*:

> The holy centaurs of the hills are vanished;
> I have nothing but the embittered sun;
> Banished heroic mother moon and vanished,
> And now that I have come to fifty years
> I must endure the timid sun.

Yeats has expressed for us in these lines the conflict of following the masculine values of power and external mastery, as seen in the sun, at the expense of banishing the moon, a traditional symbol of the feminine spirit and its values of relationships, feelings and the inner perspective.

4 The family context

The preceding discussion touched on two highly significant and related themes, those of death and the polarity of youth and old age. Both these themes are central to the mid-life crisis and indeed, a man's coming to terms with them is the cornerstone of a creative, productive outcome.

However these themes do not exist in a vacuum, in isolation; they occur and recur in the context and reality of family life. In one sense, together with birth, they constitute the reality of family life. One can think of families as if they were individuals, and as such, conceptualize them as moving through developmental crises, crises that are invariably experienced as periods of stress. Briefly, the recognizable stages of family life are the birth of the first child, the first child going to school, adolescence, 'empty nest' or when the children begin to leave the parental home, and finally, widowhood. Whilst each of these stages is a milestone in its own right, the one that holds particular relevance for, and indeed adds poignancy to, the mid-life crisis, is the stage of adolescence.

It is highly probable that during a man's mid-life transitional period at least one of his children will emerge into adolescence. What is well substantiated in psychology, primarily through the pioneering work of Erik Erikson, is that the developmental task of an adolescent is the establishment of a sense of identity; that is, to work on the task of answering the question 'Who am I?'. Failure to answer this question, or at least to find a satisfactory answer, even if temporary, results in what Erikson would call identity diffusion — in other words, being dispersed and lacking a central core; a sort of psychic dissipation that manifests itself in aimlessness. Part of establishing one's identity involves the questioning of values, invariably parental values, and reflection on the meaning and purpose of life. In other words it represents a fairly concerted effort, despite appearances to the contrary, to find some guidelines, some answer to the question 'What's it all about?'. The rawness and abrasiveness of the average teenager can often disguise the seriousness of his or her intent. It has been my experience that the average teenager is preoccupied with serious questions concerning life and death, and often feels grossly misunderstood in this pursuit.

Frequently, the questioning is accompanied by considerable angry acting out and defiant behaviour towards the authority figures of parents, since in this way does the adolescent find limits and boundaries. Hence many parents are subjected to an unceasing tirade against the very values they hold, or have held, to be of utmost importance: for example, success, security, hard work, possessions, and normal social politeness. Suddenly they find their essential meaning being violently questioned and their authority and right to make decisions being challenged. All of this is happening at the same time as the parents' mid-life crisis! It is little wonder that at the stage of adolescence, family life is turbulent and often involves violence.

It is as if the family is under siege with the consequence of a marked evocation of primitive, irrational and uncontrolled behaviour. Just as a father begins to question his life, his values, his future, one of his children is doing the same. For the father, particularly if the adolescent is a son, it is like a life-size movie of his own personal inner dilemmas. This peculiar twist of nature, this fateful similarity of process, instead of being helpful, more often than not facilitates a destructive outcome. In many ways an adolescent is an archetypal image of the mid-life crisis struggle, since he personifies the issues of youth, accentuates the threat and failure associated with age, and encapsulates the struggle for identity.

However, the precise similarity between the teenage child's dilemma and the father's mid-life crisis creates the situation where the father may see only the young person's struggles and not his own. That is, he can become overly involved, most commonly in a negative manner, with the teenager, often harshly criticizing the adolescent in a form of scape-goating behaviour. The adolescent's problems unconsciously remind him of his own difficulties, and the anxiety, fear and frustration he feels is then literally taken out on the teenager. Hence it is not only his son or daughter the father is so bitterly criticizing, it is also himself, out of his own inability to deal with the very same issues. As so often happens in life, if we do not draw a too rigid distinction between the inner and outer world, we can often witness in the outer world events and situations that correspond to our current inner difficulties. If a man in this situation can recognize the correspondence between his internal conflicts and those of his adolescent child then the possibilities of the situation being used constructively are immeasurably increased. However, much of the conflict with teenage children finds its cause in the failure of their adult parents to separate their own dilemmas from those of their children — in other words, from the failure of adults, dominated by rational thoughts, to recognize that 'outside' is so often 'inside', and 'inside' so often 'outside'. A watertight distinction, whilst giving one the comfort of distancing and the potential for blaming others, is a singularly destructive attitude in the realm of human relationships. A less rigid stance would lead to the recognition that adolescence, whilst finding its clearest expression in teenage children is, nonetheless, a universal phenomenon. The struggle for identity is a continuing struggle that we have conveniently managed to exclusively locate in teenage children. Thus in many families the mid-life crisis is hidden behind the troublesome adolescent, who in addition to his or her own identity crisis, becomes the carrier of the parents' identity struggles.

Apart from this very direct one-to-one correspondence

between the teenager's identity struggles and those of his parents, another factor contributes to the poignancy of the situation at this time in a family. This factor revolves around the personification of youthfulness that is epitomized in an adolescent. The 'hero' in our western society is the youthful person and at a primitive level in our psyche we equate youth with possibility and immortality. Whereas we equate age with finality and death. At the mid-life period, as has already been mentioned, the growing recognition of mortality collides with a powerful wish for immortality, and this wish finds its external manifestation in one's adolescent children . . . 'they have all the world before them'! The wish for immortality has the functional value of maintaining the illusions that one has created in earlier adult years, doing so, however, at the expense of reality. Death, and the awareness that one must eventually die, severely threaten us and our illusions. In addition a man's increasing awareness of his own bodily decline, and his sense of declining vitality, find stark contradiction in his teenage child.

These recognitions can produce such bitter resentment that a father becomes consumed with hatred and jealousy and finds it impossible to accept his own ageing process since he equates it with failure. This is most likely to occur where a man has not experienced a level of success achievement that measures up favourably to his earlier aspirations and dreams. Thus he feels a deep-seated sense of contempt for himself, associated with a pervasive feeling of worthlessness. In such families, constant hostility between children and their father is regrettably the norm. Other factors can serve to inflame these destructive urges, for example, a son's scholastic success, or, as in one case that I interviewed, a man's bitter resentment at paying expensive school fees (yet paradoxically, sending his children to private schools had previously served this man as a major ego-boosting status symbol).

Such resentment is partly derived from a man's inability to part with his youth and to move forward into middle adulthood. In some instances this is because, in his own family, a man has experienced a father who also was unable to move beyond this stage. In many respects we tend to get stuck at the same stage of development as our parents, since we do not have a model for progressing beyond this point. To do so, without a model, requires a very firm commitment to one's own growth and a readiness to trust the inner experience and rhythm of life. As Jung reminds us:

> The problems that crop up at this age are no longer to be solved by old recipes, the hand of this clock cannot be put back. What youth found and must find outside, the man of life's afternoon must find within himself.

The resentment and hostility projected outward onto one's adolescent children is indicative of a desire to turn the hands of the clock back. Such a desire reflects the fear of old age and death, and one's unwillingness to take the risk of going forward in the face of uncertainty.

It would be grossly inaccurate to leave an impression that difficulties in parting with youth are exclusive to men who have not achieved the desired level of success. Equally affected are the successful, the men who have often achieved success at the expense of their family and whose values, those that are associated with success, are often markedly incompatible with the adolescent's. These men may then become a target for their children's aggression and frustration as they proceed with their internal struggles. A man may therefore find himself in a peculiarly ambivalent situation. On the one hand he will want to defend his values and all that he has achieved — 'I've worked for everything I've got, and everything you (meaning the teenager) have got'. He will feel deeply resentful at having his achievements attacked and criticized. Yet the other part of him, given the nature of the mid-life crisis, will want to identify with the questioning of his values and the meaning of success. But to do so in the face of one's child's attack is a heavy demand, since a man is often frightened enough by his own crisis without running the risk, in his own eyes, of losing face in front of his children. For this admission and an ensuing dialogue to occur, the omnipotent 'hero' within the father would need to have receded, a task which may take the entire crisis to accomplish.

In addition to this conflict with one's teenage children is an even more potent experience which many men go through at this stage, one we have touched on several times: that is the realization of death. Around this stage of a man's life, on average, a man's own parents will be dying or becoming increasingly aged and in many instances disabled. The growing awareness of the ageing of one's parents, together with an awareness of the maturation of one's children, produce a sharpened and acute perception of it being one's own turn to grow old and die next. Jaques claims that this feeling about the age of parents is very strong even in people whose parents have died years before. He claims that there 'is an awareness at the mid-life period that their parents would then have been reaching old age'.

So, whether one's parents are dead, dying, or aged, it seems that the awareness of their age makes a deep impression on one's psyche and has the potent effect of reminding a man of his own mortality. 'Reminding' is a somewhat optimistic term, which belies the anxiety that such a reminder brings, since death is not a reality we manage well. Whilst we may manage to deal with the death of others, although even then we often don't cope so well, a full grasp of the certainty of one's own death is another matter. Sigmund Freud had these profound words to say about death and fantasies of immortality:

> We were prepared to maintain that death was the necessary outcome of life ... In reality however, we were accustomed to behave as if it were otherwise. We displayed an unmistakable tendency to 'shelve' death, to eliminate it from life. We tried to hush it up ... That is our own death of course ... No one believes in his own death ... In the unconscious everyone is convinced of his own immortality.

The senex of one's aged parents, combined with the puer archetype of adolescents, is sufficient to have the effect of reminding men, in a profound way, of their own mortality, even if they should wish to deny it. This reminder brings with it the recognition, very often for the first time in a man's existence, that life itself is circumscribed, has an end. This perspective of finitude has the effect of ushering in, usually with a rush, the reassessment that is so characteristic of the mid-life crisis. I cannot recall a single interview in which a man had not come to the recognition that 'time was running out'. Very often the recognition was brought into focus by the death of one's parents or, in several cases, the death, usually from cancer, of an acquaintance. As one man put it, 'If Tony could die, then I knew I could too!'.

The awareness of one's inevitable death does not result in an immediate or even quick acceptance of one's own mortality. On the contrary, the achievement of such an acceptance would signify a satisfactory resolution was close at hand. Rather does the sense of time running out lead initially to a plethora of manic, frightened activity on the one hand, or depression and inertia on the other, and in some men a cyclical fluctuation between the two. This point can often be the beginning of recurring suicidal or homicidal thoughts. For some men this awareness of mortality can have a profound effect on their everyday lives, and a spate of serious accidents, primarily car accidents, is a regular phenomenon at this stage. It is as if they wanted to bring the end of time on, rather than suffer the feeling of it 'running out'.

The first adjustment that is required of a man at this time is to accept that one is not going to achieve or be able to accomplish everything that one desired. In fact, it demands the acceptance that much will remain unfinished and many dreams unrealized. Hence, often with a sense of acute panic, the men I interviewed found themselves asking, in the words of one man, 'Is this how I want to live the rest of my life?'. Another man put the question in a different form: 'Can I make the rest of my life any more worthwhile?'. Another expressed the panic in a pessimistic vein: 'Have I had it, am I simply a failure and that's that?'.

Consistently expressed by most men were grave self-doubts and deep-seated anxieties about 'time running out'. It was this recognition that time is finite, that the infinity of youth had passed, that brought into consciousness a man's recognition that real time had also passed and that an assessment at the crossroads was both required and unavoidable. The pain of this moment can be profound, and the source of much confusion, uncertainty, anxiety and fear.

5 The occupational context

Separate from and yet not unrelated to the recognition of mortality and adolescence is a man's occupation or place of work. If there was one single theme that occurred throughout all my interviews it was the men's dissatisfaction with their current occupation. There did not seem to be a single man that I interviewed who did not express a feeling of being misplaced in his present occupation. Yet even the word 'misplaced' violates the sense of bitterness and anger that many men felt in relation to their work, and the all-encompassing feeling of one's job being one's prison.

However, upon reflection, this is precisely what one should expect of men in the mid-life crisis. This is simply because in our society a major proportion of a man's identity is derived from his work. As we have already seen a primary task of the mid-life crisis is the reworking and questioning of one's sense of identity. Returning to the adolescent parallel for a moment, it is interesting to reflect on Erik Erikson's statement that 'it is primarily the inability to settle on an occupational identity which disturbs young people'. Hence logically we could expect that the early, perhaps the very first, signs of a mid-life crisis would manifest themselves in job dissatisfaction. A man will begin to ask himself if this is what he wants to do for the remainder of his life. Several men expressed the sheer physical exhaustion that resulted from the effort they needed to make to actually keep going to work. Tiredness, boredom, depression, lethargy, and inertia characterized most of the work-orientated behaviour.

These feelings had a great deal to do with what one man described as the 'mouse in the wheel' syndrome. He expressed considerable bitterness at what he felt was now rapidly becoming to him an utterly pointless treadmill. Many men expressed deep and intense hatred toward their jobs and an overpowering feeling of resentment at being trapped. This absence of freedom, the treadmill perception, the pointlessness, all seemed to be frequently-used phrases in relation to work. These feelings, one must keep in mind, are directed towards the major source of a male's identity, so they are also the feelings he has about himself. What is perhaps somewhat surprising is that these sentiments described equally well men who were both successful and unsuccessful. The successful ones often found it a little easier to question it all than the unsuccessful ones, but the descriptions given by most men varied very little. This was also so whether they were professional or non-professional — work fundamentally was pointless for the majority of men, and one could venture a safe guess that this is valid for the majority of men in general.

The mid-life crisis is the peak point of this dissatisfaction since it is the first time men undertake a serious appraisal of the match between their dreams and reality. On the other hand, the recognition of time running out gives the matter a sense of urgency and panic. The feeling is one of 'This might be my last chance to make a big move, otherwise I will be too old'. This last sentiment reflects the dominance of the awareness of age. It became abundantly clear to me, through the interviews with this group of men, 90 per cent of whom were successful by external standards, that satisfaction in a job is not, in the final analysis, derived from such externals as salary, power and status. Many of the men I met earned high incomes but none were doing what they wanted to do.

In several situations men had occupied and held positions that represented a compromise with their own known interests. One of the major oppressions that men have been subjected to is the idea that life as a male is about having a successful career and making it in the outside world. These are the goals that a male is given during his adolescence, and in this sense a man's emotional development can be seen as being fixated at this stage, with no direction, goals or guidelines for life beyond adolescence. Men are in no way prepared for the possibility of achieving success and all its paraphernalia. Hence they are left with a pervasive feeling that it is all a massive hoax and that success is a totally vacuous notion. Such a perception contributed greatly to many of the men's feeling of betrayal, depression and futility.

Yet, upon closer scrutiny, what emerged about their occupations is that they had pursued jobs and goals that were often not of their choosing. Frequently a job or goal represented a man's parents', in particular his father's, unfulfilled ambition, his father's failed 'heroes', his father's values. In questioning their occupation seriously, men may be rebelling for the first time in a substantial way against their fathers, trying to advance their lives beyond adolescence. Is it then possible that the first adolescence is only a tepid version of the second? The tragedy is that often these men feel as powerless now as they did at 16 or so, but this time for different reasons. Now they find themselves burdened with financial responsibilities and dependants, unable to risk a change of occupation despite vehement rejection of most of the values attached to it. I think it is more than coincidence that so many men's 'heroes' are not their own, and it seems as if there is a limited period of time within which the average man is prepared to fulfil somebody else's dream, pursue somebody else's hero. The disillusionment with the first hero seems related in some instances to the death of a man's own father. Somehow along with the father's death goes the 'hero's' death, leaving a large, seemingly non-negotiable vacuum behind and ahead. It is as if the mid-life crisis brings to an end the possibility of using self-deceptive manoeuvres like 'Just one more major contract', 'The sales manager's job is what I need and then I will be happy' or 'When I get tenure I will feel more settled'.

Around 35-40 it becomes obvious to many men that these provisos are self-deceptions and that they are in fact pursuing goals or 'heroes' they no longer believe in. Reactions to the 'death' of the hero of the first half of life plus the loss of the associated goals of power, prestige and wealth, vary from a benign acceptance of the status quo through to a major restructuring of a man's life, both personal and occupational.

All of this restructuring has to take place in a social environment which is essentially hostile towards such questions. Men are not supposed to decide against a career, particularly if that career is one which society has deemed respectable and successful. Yet this set of values, which I would term the successful-career syndrome, serves to sever a man from himself, to disconnect his inner being from his outer being. Such values, somewhat ironically, reflect the very same dominance of patriarchy that has been the source of so much of women's oppression. Thus 'manhood' is achieved at a considerable distance from the reality of human relationships, from the source of subjective meaning. The meaning derived from one's occupation seems to consistently lead men to have a 'thing' or object identity, propped up by the trappings of power, with an absence of an emotional or feeling identity. To paraphrase Martin Buber, work in our western society seems to be increasingly producing in man a sense of his being in an 'it-it' relationship with the world rather than an 'I-thou' relationship. Such an orientation to the world fundamentally amounts to a man's denial of himself, since he is not 'it' but 'I'. In other words a man's subjectivity, his inner world, has been sacrificed to the outer world of success, power and competition. The words of Karl Marx, written almost 140 years ago, have astounding relevance to these thoughts and to the mid-life crisis in general:

> Labour is external to the worker, i.e. it does not belong to his essential being . . . in his work, therefore, he does not affirm himself but denies himself, does not feel content but unhappy, does not freely develop his physical and mental energy but mortifies his body and ruins his mind. The worker therefore only feels himself outside his work, and in his work feels outside himself.

> He is at home when he is not working, and when he is
> working he is not at home.

Whilst the temptation is to label Marx's ideas as having relevance only to the proletariat, their relevance to the issues discussed in connection with work and the mid-life crisis is undeniable, since in a world that has material success as its God and *raison d'être*, we are all proletariat — whether professional or non-professional, white or blue collar, is beside the point. With advances in technology the phenomenon of work being 'outside', external to man, is an ever-increasing and dominant factor. Finer and finer divisions of labour have left many men with a strong sense of technical competence and an even stronger sense of human incompetence. These two factors co-exist with the ever present possibility of redundancy for many males of the 35-45 years age-group. Alongside this exists the reality of an uncompromisingly harsh atmosphere of competition that finally separates not only men from their families, and men from men, but man from himself, from the very source of his own humanity.

Such a separation can affect various aspects of a man's life. Inwardly it leads to a chronic sense of loss and associated feelings of grief. Not only does a man inevitably feel the deep sense of loss in relation to the passing of his youth that we discussed earlier, in the family context; he also feels, although not consciously, the loss of aspects of himself, loss of contact with and experience of his inner world of being. The natural reaction to a sense of loss is grief, and although we tend to think of grief only as a reaction to death, such a tendency detracts from a broader understanding of this emotion. Just as we have conveniently assigned the adolescence phenomenon exclusively to the realm of a teenager, thus facilitating the denial of its general and universal qualities, so also have we managed a similar process with grief. We think of grieving and mourning as being exclusively related to physical death, whereas in reality the grief that is seen as a reaction to death is merely its clearest manifestation. Equally so is grief the reaction to the loss or passing of anything — event, person or whatever — that we value.

54

Hence for a man in the mid-life period, with the prevailing loss of youth, of a sense of meaning and of contact with his inner world, plus the awareness of his own mortality, one can readily understand how grief and grieving would characterize his emotional life. In fact whenever the predictability of events, the routine meaning of events, has been invalidated or disturbed, this loss of meaning will bring about a process of bereavement. The very process of change itself, biologically and psychologically determined as it is in mid-life crises, is a sufficient condition for evoking a deep sense of loss and producing a grief reaction. However, unlike the mourning that accompanies the death of a relative or friend, the grief accompanying change is not supported by custom, is not rendered acceptable. Whilst to mourn for one's deceased relatives is socially acceptable and indeed a clearly articulated and spelt out form of behaviour, to mourn for the loss of oneself is an alien, unsupported grief. Such is the grief of the mid-life crisis, an inexplicable, unacceptable, unrecognized grief, since what is mourned is not seen as having been lost. Many men would think it verging on the insane if one suggested to them that they were mourning for the sense of loss, both inner and outer, of youthfulness. Yet, not only are they mourning for this, they have also often lost their dreams, lost the possibility of fulfilling their hopes and ambitions: in other words they are mourning the passing of their Siegfried, their hero.

To deny that they are experiencing grief is a predictable reaction, as would be a man's denial that he was going through a second adolescence, since the rational, logical mind cannot accept such propositions. Moreover for men, with their heavy social conditioning to be logical and rational, it is especially difficult to accept the idea that they may be experiencing grief. But if we examine the typical signs of grief it will be abundantly clear that the pattern of grief is replicated in the mid-life crisis, or for that matter in any period of major change.

A clear summary of these typical signs is given by Peter Marris:

> ... physical distress and worse health; an inability to surrender the past — expressed for instance, by brooding

over memories, sensing the presence of the dead, clinging to possessions, being unable to comprehend the loss, feelings of unreality; withdrawal into apathy; and hostility against others, against fate, or turned in upon oneself.

It is this pattern, particularly the 'inability to surrender the past', that characterizes the mid-life situation; to surrender the past means to surrender one's youth, to surrender one's hopes, aspirations and dreams that now need to be modified. The 'clinging to possessions' we have already discussed as being characteristic of men in whom the physical dimension predominated. The 'withdrawal into apathy' is a frequent pattern, expressing itself in the mid-life crisis as 'What's the point of it all?'. 'Hostility against others' we have already discussed as being a regular pattern in the relationship between adolescent children and their mid-life crisis father. Equally we will see, a little further on, that hostility directed towards wives is common. Of general significance is the characteristic of 'being unable to comprehend the loss'. This inability has already been discussed in relation to male oppression. One of the tools of this oppression is indoctrination with the success goal; hence to achieve this goal yet still to feel a sense of loss, is incomprehensible to most men. There do not exist any customs, or rites of passage, for the loss that occurs in the mid-life period, hence there does not exist any means of making sense of the grief. As one man said, 'I just couldn't understand what was happening to me, I thought maybe I was going crazy; nothing made sense to me any more'. Or, in the words of another, 'I had made all this money, I had felt more success than I ever expected and I still felt rotten, I couldn't make head or tail of it'.

Example after example could be given, all of which would only serve to confirm that grief, grieving and the mid-life crisis could be seen as symptomatically representing a period of prolonged mourning. Again Peter Marris provides a very useful comment on grief and highlights its relationship to the mid-life period when he says:

Grief then, is the expression of a profound conflict between contradictory impulses — to consolidate all that is still valuable and important in the past and preserve it from loss; and at the same time, to re-establish a meaningful pattern of relationships in which the loss is accepted.

These thoughts regarding the conflict between contradictory impulses are very relevant to any discussion on the mid-life period, since in the simplest possible terms the mid-life conflict is between holding on to the past and its successes and letting go, in order to move forward.

However, one or two factors complicate the progress of mourning in this period of life. Normally one could expect mourning to extend over a period of approximately two years. By this time, to re-quote Marris, 'a meaningful pattern of relationships in which the loss is accepted' would be established. But as has already been pointed out a major difficulty in the mid-life crisis is that it is often difficult for a man to know what has been lost. Hence if one does not know what one has lost, but only has the sense of loss, it is difficult to resolve the conflict. Perhaps it is a little like the difficulties in mourning that result when a person is simply declared to be 'presumed dead' and a body, an actual body, is never found. It is harder for the relatives in these situations to satisfactorily mourn, since the hope, the wish, that the person is still alive can be maintained. (This is not unlike the wish for immortality that we have discussed already.) Because there is nothing substantial to bury, the wish can, to an extent, be maintained, but at the expense of a satisfactory working through of the grief. So, for the male going through the mid-life crisis, the lack of evidence does complicate the mourning. The fact that such a person does not know what he has lost — at a simple level his youth and, at a deeper level, his sense of self — prolongs the mourning process and inhibits the re-establishment of meaning and the restructuring of one's personal life that has already been mentioned as a critical task of the mid-life period.

Another complicating factor derives from the known fact that mourning is aided, the grieving more successful, when the mourner's life has been composed of a number of meaningful personal relationships. Another way of expressing this is by saying that if a mourner's major, if not exclusive source of identity, is tied up with the deceased person, the grieving is likely to remain unresolved. A parallel to this situation can be readily seen in the male mid-life crisis when one recollects how a man's sense of identity in our society is predominantly derived from his occupation. Thus, when this fails to satisfy him, fails to give him a sense of identity, his major source of meaning is removed and he can, like the overly-dependent widow, experience chronic, unresolved grief. I believe this is the case with many men in, and after, the mid-life crisis. They find themselves in a state of prolonged depression or, as Geoffrey Gorer has called it, 'mummification' — that is, life is frozen at the moment of loss, unable to move forward — and rather than turn the hands of the clock back, some men simply resort to stopping them. At this point they can be seen as having inadvertently chosen to die since as Jung so appositely said: 'From the middle of life onward, only he remains vitally alive who is ready to die with life'. To not make this choice, to not move forward with the natural rhythm of the seasons of life, is an unwillingness to 'die with life'. The actual physical death of such men can be seen as simply an explicit statement of what has implicitly occurred, on the average, 30 years previously, when they failed to make the choice and thereby died psychologically.

Another aspect or feature of grieving that is often mentioned in discussions on grief, but which has not been discussed here as yet, is a particular phase of mourning characterized by the 'if onlys' — for example 'If only I had called the doctor earlier', or more poignantly, 'If only I had said — or hadn't said — such and such'. Generally the 'if only' phase is indicative of the individual concerned trying to appease the mixture of depression, anger and guilt he or she feels. Temporarily it can have the seemingly paradoxical effect of increasing the guilt, but in a way this self-punishment has the effect, at the same time, of absolving the person from the heavy sense of responsibility he or she feels.

With regard to the mid-life crisis it is possible to see this 'if only' stage operating in the grief that men are experiencing. Whilst granting that the following is but one possible interpretation of events, it does seem to fit the experience of the

58

men I interviewed. In essence, it appears that if a man has accepted his loss, has recognized that many dreams etc. are not going to be fulfilled, and has accepted the burden of his own mortality, then his grieving will progress to the stage of 'if only'. He may find himself saying 'If only I had done this', 'If only I had made the decision to take that particular position', or perhaps 'If only I had stayed at school'. However, accompanying this type of 'if only' is another variation that has to do with seeking a resolution to the inner sense of despair. This takes the pattern of fantasies about what one would be like 'if only' and represents a sort of inner escape from the depression, an escape that is often both necessary and healthy. It is as if the fantasy life is trying to point the way forward, trying to assist the process of re-establishing meaning and to facilitate the integration of loss. Four fantasies occurred regularly amongst the men I interviewed, and from clinical experience it seems to me that these four are expressions of a recurring phenomenon in men in general.

The farmer fantasy: By far the most regularly-occurring fantasy was 'If only I were a farmer'. To own, run and live on a farm or farmlet, to belong to the land, to know the pace of nature and the rhythm of animals: this was the most prevalent fantasy. Men, as they mourn the loss of youth and old heroes, seem to regularly escape into the farmer fantasy; rarely did the men I interviewed seem to grasp the reality of toil and sweat associated with actually being a farmer. Rather theirs was an idyllic picture that had far more to do with a man's desire to sense his own inner self and its rhythm, than it had to do with any actual reality of being a farmer. Each man that shared this fantasy with me did so with an acute sense of embarrassment, a sort of 'Now you will think I'm silly' type of attitude. Yet this fantasy can be the very key to a man's resolution of the mid-life crisis. I hasten to add that this does not mean the actual fulfilment of the dream of becoming a farmer, since as a real solution it is both remote and probably undesirable. Rather the secret lies in exploring the inner meaning of the fantasy, the meaning of the symbols to the individual, and then attempting a change in one's actual situation in the light of this inner meaning. For example, if this fantasy expresses, as I suspect it did on most occasions, a man's desire to restore and literally cultivate his own sense of natural rhythm and freedom as personified in rural life, then these yearnings are the ones needing an opportunity for expression in everyday life.

Having said that, it is equally applicable to view each of the other fantasies from the same perspective, although each of them in turn represents different inner struggles and meanings.

The nurseryman fantasy: The second most regular fantasy was 'If only I were a nurseryman'. This is not unrelated to the farmer fantasy although its central meaning has more to do with nurturing and growth. The desire or wish to be a nurseryman seems to be more common amongst professionals than non-professionals. It seems that this fantasy relates to a man's inner need to care for and promote the growth of living things; to a need to escape the harsh reality, the demands of people, so often experienced by men in professional positions. For some, to set up a plant nursery appeared feasible; however, as with the 'farmer', to realize the fantasy can run the risk of attempting an external solution to an internal problem. That is not to say that some men would not be happier as nurserymen — they may well be; but the critical task as I see it is to recognize what the inner meaning of this fantasy is, and to further accept that outside is inside and inside, outside. Therefore the fantasy has a great deal to do with a man's wish for inner growth and his need for self-care and nurturing. Perhaps in the simplest of terms the fantasy of being a nurseryman reflects a man's inner need to be 'watered', 'fertilized', 'weeded' and generally cared for! It is in exploring this inner meaning, as has already been suggested, that the key to resolution lies. For once a man understands the meaning, he can then make realistic plans for bringing about a change in his life style that will result in these inner needs being met. Often these are the very needs that have been sacrificed in obtaining and securing the successes of the first half of life. Hence they tend to be emotional, to do with feelings rather than actions.

The helper fantasy: A third regularly occurring fantasy was that of being a helper, someone who in a general sense 'wants to help people'; this fantasy not infrequently took the specific form of a desire to do social work or some allied activity. Again, it is quite possible that some men could fulfil this fantasy, and I firmly believe that many should be encouraged to do so. Just as the 'nurseryman' tended to come from professional groups, the 'social work' pattern was most predominant amongst self-made, successful businessmen, many of whom expressed a desire to give something back to the community. This desire, in itself, was absolutely genuine, however the irony is that often these men have sacrificed the well-being of their own families in the pursuit of their materialistic goals; in such cases the fantasy has as much to do with attempting reparation and meeting needs for warm and caring relationships, as it has to do with a genuine desire to help others. It was difficult not to arrive at the conclusion that the longing to be able to help others was fundamentally about the inner need for a close, intimate relationship which would provide the man with an opportunity to both care and be cared for. With this understanding, it is likely that some men could simply modify their immediate lives in order to meet the need, whereas others may well find their way into social work or some equivalent. However, it is to be hoped that the latter group would also both recognize and accept the inner meaning of their fantasy.

The writer fantasy: The fourth 'if only' was the fantasy of being a writer or some other creative person, although a writer was the predominant one. Those men whose lives were lived mostly on the intellectual plane tended to predominate in this group. Here the fantasy was of writing the 'great work', which was in most cases a great novel, not a definitive text. These men believed that 'If only I could write full time then my misery and unhappiness would disappear'. Again, for some of these men, the possibility of writing was not unlikely, for others it was remote; but the essential point is the inner meaning, the inner message, being conveyed by the fantasy.

A noticeable characteristic amongst intellectually orientated men is the lop-sided development of their psyche. Logic and rational thought have been accentuated and developed at the expense of the irrational, intuitive and creative aspects. Hence the fantasy of being a writer, or for that matter any other sort of artist, has to do with an inner demand, arising around the mid-life period, to give some time and space to the neglected sides of one's psyche. This particular fantasy expresses the inner drive to be creative and to experience an alternative mode to the rational, empirical, logical mode. Amongst some men, it was the acquisition of musical skills that formed their fantasy. Indeed, it is not uncommon to find a new interest in music being developed by men in their mid-thirties to mid-forties. This may simply take the form of listening, or, as in some instances, it may take the form of desiring to learn to play an instrument. Again, several men I interviewed had this desire, but were strongly inclined to dismiss it and not take it seriously. This is a grave error since the desire represents an inner prompting, a reminder of needed growth, an inner direction for partly resolving, in a creative way, the mid-life crisis. Frequently the dismissal of the idea was motivated by the old attitudes of the first half of life, such as fear of failure. But to allow this or any other archaic attitude such as 'I'm too old now' to inhibit these urges, is to deny oneself the possibility of growth. To deny such possibilities is, as has already been discussed, to sentence oneself to death and to allow oneself to be captured like an insect in a web of inertia. This self-spun inertia is derived from the altered sense of time that comes with the mid-life period: the awareness of 'time running out' can lead to the inertia of 'it's too late to start anything'.

These four fantasies, although not the only fantasies men have, nevertheless represent a sufficiently repetitive pattern to warrant the attention they were given. However, whatever the fantasy about what one would like to do, it warrants attention simply because it is an individual's own fantasy, his creation out of his psyche, and therefore potentially a key to the modification and restructuring required in the second half of life. In short, it is the beginning of the construction of a new 'hero'. A man's battle will be to actually manage to trust the fantasy long enough to explore its meaning. The well-learned lessons of logic and rationality will be felt and experienced as a powerful force insisting on its dismissal as a 'silly daydream'. 'Daydream' maybe, but 'silly' no, unless one is so entrenched in the outer masculine world as to regard all the inner world as silly. To hold such a position perhaps reflects fear as much as anything else, fear of the world of emotions and feelings, fear of getting out of control. For men with this outlook, the mid-life crisis is the nervous blink, rather than the prolonged stare, a stare that may make visible a renewed and truly personal purpose for being alive.

However it is known from bereavement and grieving studies that the abortion of the grief process, which will be the pattern in men denying their own inner life, the 'nervous blinkers' so to speak, has definitive consequences. Fundamentally this pattern in bereavement represents the impulse to escape from everything, to deny that one feels sad and lost and to ward off such feelings by engaging in a heightened level of activity, a sort of 'busy-bee syndrome'. The same sort of pattern is seen in men who avoid the inner reality and its meaning for them during the mid-life crisis. Ironically it is not those who listen and take cognizance of their fantasy or daydreams who are escaping, but rather those who do not listen and who dismiss the inner world; perhaps, as has already been suggested, physical menopause is these men's 'Waterloo'!

Dropping out fantasy: Another feature of the grieving process that seems to relate to the mid-life crisis and is not unrelated to the 'escapism' that has just been discussed, is the tendency amongst some men to act out their crisis by simply 'dropping out'. For many men, on the other hand, the idea of dropping out remains in the realm of fantasy, the desert island type of fantasy (or the west coast of California fantasy if you happen to be an American). Most of the men holding the 'desert island' type of drop-out fantasy recognized it as fantasy and did not seriously consider it would solve their problems. However a slightly more reality-based drop-out fantasy, related to a strong sense of wanting to re-create a meaningful pattern, does occur in many men. Their fantasies represent an attempt

63

to reconstruct a radically different sense of self through a drastic change of occupation. Hence to find men acting out their identity crisis by a major change of job around 35-45 is a recognizable pattern of mid-life. Within the change is the hope that it will bring an end to the inner sense of pain and confusion. Many men of 35-45 experience restlessness and seek a position that appears uncomplicated and simple. This is a reaction against the sense of competition, aggression and pressure that has dominated much of their work life. Such a change can work, so long as the decision is made at the right stage of the crisis. By way of analogy, one can think of individuals who make drastic changes in their lives within a few months of their partner dying. What one can say with confidence about such behaviour is that it is too early and prevents the working through of grief. However if the changes were to begin at a later stage, for example, any time after 12 months after the death of one's partner, then one would tend to see them as a healthy process at work.

This same model can be applied to men undergoing the mid-life crisis with respect to their desire and wish to bring about a major change in their lives. To fantasize about simply dropping out is basically a solution destined to fail, since its motivation is one of avoiding the necessary mourning of loss. To drop out and become what one might call a 'mid-life hippie', is behaviour that basically repeats the methods used by a man for handling his first adolescence. Erikson, in discussing teenage adolescence says: 'Youth after youth, bewildered by some assumed role, a role forced on him by the inexorable standardization of American adolescence, runs away in one form or another; leaving schools and jobs, staying out all night, or withdrawing into bizarre and inaccessible moods'. One can readily see the direct relevance of this description to men in the mid-life transition, as they run away from the 'inexorable standardization' of the 'successful male' and the enforced role that this imposes upon them. 'Dropping out' then is the mid-life equivalent of 'running away', and whilst it provides immediate relief from the depression and anxiety, the operative point is that by and large the relief will only be temporary. This is simply because an unavoidable demand of the crisis is the working through of the sense of loss; dropping out merely delays the working through and in all probability, within a period of six months, the distractions and attractions of dropping out will have begun to fail in their capacity to delay the grieving. Dropping out totally is too severe a shock and trauma to the male psyche, given the years of conditioning and learning that have led to a male's sense of having an occupation as such. It tends to be too abrupt a transition which aborts the natural process of working through a crisis. However at the level of fantasy, thoughts of a desert island get many a man through a bad mid-life crisis day! One can safely assume that it is a very rare man indeed who can respond creatively and productively to dropping out and that such a man is probably dropping out *to* something rather than *from* something. It is also probable that such successful dropping out is well timed in so far as it does not represent an abortion of the grieving process, an early and premature panic reaction to the mid-life crisis, but rather a carefully timed conclusion to the crisis.

This brings us to the second type of acting-out of fantasy, which is to do not with dropping out *per se*, but with a major change in occupation. For many men the reassessment of goals, priorities and values that we have so often discussed, leads to a decision to make a major change of occupation. If this decision emerges as a conclusion or resolution to the grief, that is the depression has been accepted and worked through, then such a decision can represent a substantial step in the direction of re-establishing one's sense of identity. It is not uncommon for this major change to involve consider-able risk and it can quite often take the form of wanting to be self-employed and to develop one's own business along lines consistent with a man's interests. Such a choice can signify a creative illness process in the sense we have already discussed, since it represents a resolution, a moving forward. Other men may simply yearn for a change of job, but if this yearning is for an occupation that is basically inconsistent and incompatible with their needs, then such a change will not produce any permanent solution. In essence however, the impetus to change should be recognized as reflecting a deeper sense of unrest, and its full meaning for the individual should be explored by allowing the ideas and feelings to be aired in the light of consciousness. That is, they should be felt, thought and talked about and not dismissed as simply restlessness. A man's occupation, rightly or wrongly, is the cornerstone of his identity: hence stirrings and rumblings about his occupation are stirrings and rumblings about himself. To ignore, dismiss, and not listen to or take a sounding of such movement, is to deny the existence of a stirring and restlessness that is far broader and more profound than simply one's occupation. Such denial can only lead to a further abortion of the grieving process and the failure to develop and sustain the creative features and aspects of the mid-life crisis. Fundamentally this denial is a failure to accept and move with change, a desire to stop the hands of the clock, since change itself is perceived as a threat, not an opportunity. Men who choose this alternative are in essence choosing to live their lives in 'half-obscurity', to use a Kierkegaardian phrase, a life lived for purposes other than one's own.

6 Marriage and the mid-life crisis

We have now seen how a man's mid-life crisis can both have ramifications, and manifest itself, in his relationship with his adolescent children and in the occupational sphere. The adolescent arena captures the inner polarity of youthfulness versus age, or possibility versus finitude, whilst the occupational realm is the context in which a man's identity crisis finds its most powerful expression, since in our society what a man does has been inextricably bound up with who he is. For many men this joining has been disastrous and has prevented their finding out who actually lives behind the persona. In many ways this reflects the problem with all roles — that they serve to both hide us from ourselves and give us somewhere to hide ourselves from others. The mid-life transition is a period when an inner tension and discontent can arise about this game of hide-and-seek. As we have already discussed, work not only separates men from each other and from their families but also man from himself. It facilitates, and often actually encourages, the externalization of himself and the severance between his inner and outer worlds in such a way that he literally becomes a stranger to himself. As one man said when speaking of his crisis: 'It was so unlike me, I had never been like this before, it was almost as if it wasn't me'.

It is inevitable that when one loses a sense of oneself,

loses the sense of 'who I am', the capacity to sustain ongoing intimate relationships will be impaired. Since the vast majority of men around 35 are married, or have been, it is to be expected that the other major area of their lives to be disturbed and to experience a crisis will be their marriage. It is a common phenomenon that many, if not most marriages, regardless of their supposed level of happiness, will experience a major period of disturbance between the tenth and fifteenth year of existence. Whilst it is perfectly valid to assert that all marriages experience periods of disturbance throughout their existence, I nevertheless believe that this tenth-to-fifteenth year period is a time of specific and very critical disturbance. This phenomenon is related to the fact that both partners will, as individuals, be experiencing aspects of the mid-life transition. Although this book is specifically concerned with the male mid-life crisis, much of which has been discussed is equally applicable to females, since they also undergo a mid-life transition and whilst the context varies from the male crisis, the process is similar. This is simply because the actual process of change does not vary regardless of what the content of the change is about. This disturbance can take the form of minor irritation through to actual divorce, but at both ends of the spectrum and throughout the range, is a consistent sense of boredom and aimlessness accompanied by a serious questioning of the purpose and point of the marriage. Whilst for many couples this questioning is extremely anxiety-provoking because it collides head-on with their long-held fantasies of what marriage is about, others are able to perceive the crisis as an opportunity for growth and not solely a threat.

As has already been mentioned this period of disturbance in a marriage coincides with the mid-life crisis of both the husband and the wife. This in itself is sufficient to precipitate the marital crisis and warrants a full discussion in its own right. However, before this is done, another factor that contributes to the crisis ought to be discussed, since it forms the background of the mid-life interaction. This factor can be broadly conceived as mate-choice, although such a label tends to oversimplify the dynamics. There are several ways in which this topic can be approached, however as this book is not concerned with mate-choice *per se*, it is preferable to restrict the discussion to the mid-life transition. In this regard one need simply state that the reasons individuals have for marrying each other, and thus for staying married to each other, have a limited life. By this I mean that the dream, vision, or in the terms of this book, the hero or heroine, is not immortal and indeed will die. For some individuals barely six months will elapse before the fantasy with which they entered marriage, the vision or dream that they held about this marriage and their partner, will be shattered. In other marriages this process of disillusionment takes much longer to occur, however it is doubtful if in any marriage the original reason, or reasons, for marrying a person can sustain the marriage much beyond a decade. I am not here talking of the minor, advice-column type of disillusionments that occur from the beginning of and throughout a marriage. What I am referring to is the basic motivation — a large part of which we are totally unware, since it is unconscious — behind one person's marrying another: in other words the *raison d'être* of a marriage. It is inconceivable that the original reasons could last beyond ten years since by then the two individuals, as individuals, would have undergone considerable change through the sheer passage of time. In addition ten years of exposure to each other would have revealed a substantial amount more about one's partner than was available at the time of marriage. Mind you it is equally true to say that ten years of marriage can result in such a habitual manner of relating that we fail to see any new information about our partner. However, the central point is that the reasons, both conscious and unconscious, for initiating a marriage and maintaining it for the first ten years or so, will simply prove insufficient and inadequate to sustain it for the second decade.

One has to find a new reason for staying married, if the two alternatives of divorce and mediocrity are to be avoided. In many ways what is called for is an inner divorce, a divorce or separation from the early and often immature reason for being married, followed by a remarriage to one's partner. This is often the process that individuals go through on the outside of themselves; that is, when they reach this *ennui* period in a marriage they seek an external divorce and remarriage to another person. In many situations this is the appropriate solution, since the marriage has been entered into on questionable grounds, and the continuance of an empty marriage is a destructive act for all persons involved. These instances are often marriages where the reasons for marrying had more to do with unconscious negative feelings about one's parents, and as a consequence the marital inter-action becomes an arena for a replay of the parent/child interaction. Divorce and separation in these situations in which the marriage is characterized by highly destructive behaviour is often a healthy choice. However, I have often wondered how many marriages end in an inappropriate divorce. By this I simply mean that they ended in an external, legal, separation and divorce, when really what the couples were struggling with was this *ennui* period of a marriage, and an inner divorce might be seen as more appropriate.

Perhaps this will be clearer if I explain in a little more detail what I mean by this notion. Behind it is the assump-tion that in marriage the cement or adhesive that holds it together is a set of mutual projections. That is we tend to see and put onto our partner what we cannot see or accept about ourselves. For example, if a man cannot accept his feelings of inadequacy because his father and mother always criticized him and made him feel bad, he may well display a tendency to be very critical of his wife and see her as being grossly inadequate. That is, he will project, just like a movie projector, these scenes or aspects within himself that he cannot deal with, or accept, onto his wife. Their interaction will be characterized by a dominant, aggressive, over-confident husband and a submissive, oppressed and lacking-in-confidence wife. This will in all probability 'suit' the wife psychologically for a period of time, since she may well have been brought up in such a way that she learned to distrust and not accept her own competence and to feel inadequate; hence she in turn projects her competence onto her husband. For many females this description is an accurate one, since as females they have been taught that competence was unfeminine and to be equated with masculine, whilst for men to experience feelings, particularly feelings of inadequacy, was equated with being feminine. This description also provides an apposite example of the reason, or at least one of them, for staying married; a reason that in the interests of self-maturation ought not continue, and certainly not last beyond the first half of life.

Another example, one that is perhaps even more relevant in the context of the present discussion, is found in the marriage where the wife literally carries the feeling aspects of the marriage and the husband the thinking aspects. The feeling function thereby is projected onto the woman. In our society it is this projection, along with that of the competence/incompetence aspect, that tends to occur most regularly in marriage. This is simply because our society has such rigid and limited notions of male/female that these broader social role expectations actively facilitate such projections and counter-projections. In those marriages where the male carries the logic or thinking projection, he has learnt that to have and express feelings is equivalent to being irrational and to be irrational is bad and weak. As has already been discussed it is in this learning that the nucleus of attitudes that work against a satisfactory resolution of the male mid-life crisis is to be found. Many men, as soon as they come to equate the inner world with irrationality, learn to fear it as being a sign of weakness and regard it as an unacceptable part of themselves. Hence it is projected onto the female. This is the aspect which Jung would call the *anima*, the so-called feminine aspects of a man. The female in turn has been socialized into believing that thinking is a male function, 'something females are no good at'. Thus she has learned to equate thinking and logic with masculinity and therefore can emotionally reject these components or aspects of herself and project them onto her partner.

Thus the marriage itself represents one complete person and the respective partners a half each. At this stage, which is almost invariably in the first 10-15 years of marriage, the marriage will be basically harmonious provided the adjustment is satisfactory in other respects. This harmony is derived from the mutual projections which function as a type of emotional cement. One can see that in many respects this could be a perfectly satisfactory harmony, particularly since it coincides with that phase in a man's life when mastery, success and achievement in the outer world form his major goals. However, one major disadvantage sooner or later will emerge into one or both partners' consciousness, and that is that they are only complete as a pair but not as individuals. The other half of them has been located in, projected onto, their partner. The emergence of this awareness, I would argue, is inevitable and heralds the beginning of the critical phase of a marriage. This newly-recognized source of disturbance is the very feature that had held the marriage together and given it meaning. This loss of meaning is central to the marriage crisis at this mid-point period (just as it was to the mid-life crisis of the men I interviewed).

If indeed this view of marriage — one in which half of each individual is tied up in his or her partner — has validity, then clearly what is required if individual growth is to occur is a separation, an inner, not outer separation, from one's partner. It is a paradox that intimacy itself may well only be achieved as a result of a period of separation. By re-owning and reclaiming those previously lost aspects of ourselves we move towards completion and a clearer sense of identity. In doing so we become progressively more capable of intimacy, since it no longer poses the threat of submerging us. Hence my view that an inner or psychological separation or divorce from habitual and outmoded ways of perceiving each other may well be the appropriate step for many couples who would otherwise seek the solution external to themselves, in a legal divorce. If this inner divorce and separation can be achieved then a new *raison d'être* can be gradually formed to replace the old and more immature one of the first half of life. However it may well be that despite the extreme trauma and difficulties involved, a legal divorce would nevertheless prove to be a less difficult alternative than this process of inner separation or divorce. The latter demands a commitment to one's individual growth, and a willingness to look in and seek the answer. As Jung so clearly reminds us: 'Seldom or never does a marriage develop into an individual relationship smoothly

72

and without crises. There is no birth of consciousness without pain.'

In other words there is no development of the inner self, no movement towards completion, without crises and pain. Yet it is this that many individuals want to avoid, in particular the painful process of inner divorce and separation that is the necessary prerequisite to remarriage to the same partner. That is, some separation leading to a clearer sense of our own individuality is required before we can develop a renewed reason for being married — and in this sense being remarried — to our existing partners as they are and not as we need them to be.

It would be easy to misconstrue what I have said and take it to mean that marriages cannot and will not last beyond 10-15 years. Whilst this has the appeal of sensationalism it would be a complete distortion of my view. What I am saying is that the initial reasons, the initial motivation, for getting married and staying married, will be unlikely to be appropriate and useful much beyond ten years. But implicit in this assertion is the assumption that marriage is not necessarily only about well-being or comfort, but is also about the challenge of completing oneself, of reclaiming the projected, externalized aspects of self, of re-owning the 'other half'. For this to occur a crisis is inevitable, but it can be and ought to be a creative crisis, leading to an expanded awareness of self. Contrary to the negative view that marriages will only last for ten or 15 years, I would argue that marriage provides one of the best opportunities within which this movement towards a person's unfolding can occur. To seek external solutions to the crisis may well be inappropriate in many situations; furthermore, to rush into a legal outer divorce may well be an escape from the inevitable suffering that accompanies and sets the scene for growth. It is becoming increasingly fashionable, following the leadership of American family sociologists, to believe that we need different partners for different stages of life, one for the pre-child stage, a different one for the child-rearing stage and then one to retire with. The view of marriage propounded in this chapter so far is in agreement with the idea of different marriages at different stages of life; my only disagreement is that I hold the view that where possible these different marriages ought to be to the same person. Academics, and sociologists in particular, show a peculiar affinity with the outside world and manage to maintain a rigid distinction between outside and inside, between the macro and micro. The concept of different marriages to the same person is an 'inside' view that recognizes inside is outside and outside is inside. However the one essential prerequisite for internal remarriages is that both partners be willing to accept the challenge and all that it entails.

A further complicating factor is that while both may be willing to accept the challenge, they may be so at different times. In general women seem to arrive at the mid-life crisis earlier than men, which reflects the strength of the resistance that men have towards listening to their inner world of emotions. Whilst both partners may go through the crisis at a similar time, they very often start it at different times and move through it at a different pace. Such differences in tempo seem to be more often the norm than the exception, and a source of considerable anxiety. Jung makes the following comment on this phenomenon:

> These differences in tempo and in the degree of spiritual development are the chief causes of a typical difficulty which makes its appearance at critical moments.

By 'spiritual' Jung means a 'certain complexity of mind or nature, comparable to a gem with many facets as opposed to a simple cube'. This is similar to my use of the phrase 'moving towards completion'. The 'degree of spiritual development', then, refers to the differences in stages of evolution or completion of the individual partners; very often this evolution is out of phase and a source of tension. Both the male mid-life crisis and the frequently accompanying mid-marriage crisis provide the opportunity to reject the limited view of oneself as a 'simple cube' and accept the unceasing task of unearthing the 'gem' that is truly one's Self.

Female mid-life crisis: Although this book is solely concerned with the male mid-life crisis it is nevertheless necessary to focus a little on the counterpart in females, since in most instances the male crisis is acted out in the male-female context. Whilst the material for the present book was derived from specific interviews with males, I have, in the course of several years of counselling, had access to the feelings of women undergoing this period in their lives and it is from this clinical experience that the present comments are derived.

What is reasonably well established these days is that the majority of married females will have completed their child-bearing years by the age of 30 and that hence their last child will be going to school by the time they approach 35 years of age. Given normal life expectancy, this leaves some 35-40 years of adult life which will not be exclusively bound up with children. What is equally well established by family psychologists, drawing on the idea of the family life-cycle that we discussed in relation to men and their adolescent children, is that the time of the last child going to school can constitute a critical stage. Women at this point can experience an overwhelming sense of being in a vacuum with no sense of which way to move in their lives. It is as if having had their heads literally buried in the task of motherhood, they have forgotten who it is who is the mother! That is, just like men's occupations, the role of motherhood can be so all-consuming and devouring that the identity becomes fused with the role and women find it difficult to respond and recognize any aspects of themselves that do not answer to the name 'Mum'. The last child going to school can constitute a crisis since this parting represents a dislocation of a woman's sense of equilibrium: interruptions of this nature frequently constitute a crisis. Whilst it is perfectly true that some women do not experience it as a crisis and have either managed to continue an occupation external to their role as wife and mother, or alternatively have thoroughly prepared for this period in their lives, it is my impression that for a large number of women it remains a very difficult time. For each woman will feel divided: a part of her will want to return to the work force, yet another part will experience acute panic and fear at this thought, panic and fear derived from a deeply-felt sense of inadequacy, a sort of institutional neurosis!

This external time-sequence of the last child going to school often coincides with the internal one of a woman's inner promptings at a time of her mid-life crisis. The pervasive sense of vacuum she either anticipates, or actually experiences, provides the necessary, albeit at times fearful, space within which a woman can reflect on her situation. This reflection may focus on many things, but two areas that quite clearly emerge are those of her marriage and herself. In a sense her 'dreams' come up for review and for many women the review is felt as a negative experience, a disillusioning feeling, that can lead to a marked sense of depression and hopelessness. This process is by no means exclusively the concern of married women with children. On the contrary it is inevitable that women, whether single or married, with or without children, will find themselves undertaking a review around the ages of 30-35. For unmarried women this can be a review about whether to continue in their career, to continue to be an achiever or not. In this sense this stage is identical with aspects of the male crisis; however for such women an additional variable can often be the question of reconciling these interests with the seemingly conflicting issues of whether to be married and have children. For married women without children the review can bring into sharp focus the question of whether to have children or not. This situation can frequently have a compulsive 'now or never' quality about it. Actual free choice is made fairly difficult by the fact that, despite some improvement, it is still generally regarded as 'abnormal' to be married and choose not to have children; traditional heroines are alive and well! But just as we saw in relation to men, the death of the hero, or in this situation the heroine, and the attendant state of disillusionment, may well be the necessary and unavoidable conditions for a mid-life crisis. Perhaps the sense of hopelessness and pointlessness that is glimpsed for the first time when one's normal level of activity slows down signifies the commencement of the transition period.

For women a lot of the discontent is concerned with a sense of resentment at having been heavily defined in the nurturing, caring role, and not having developed a sense of competence and mastery external to themselves. That is, they feel frustrated in their need for a sense of achievement. If a man's need is to remove himself from the heavy external emphasis and to correct this with an emphasis on the internal or inside aspects, a woman's need appears to be the reverse. She very often will feel a strong desire to be known as competent, but more fundamentally, to be simply known, by people other than her husband and children: that is to have a sense of herself which is separate from, and additional to, that of 'Mrs So-and-so' and 'Mum'. This is identical to the male dilemma of wanting to define himself in additional ways to that of his occupation. As we will discuss in further detail in a later chapter, this inner prompting and stirring in women is the emergence of what Jung would term the *animus,* that part of the female psyche that has to do with the spirit of mastery. As with men, the emergence of this inner aspect with its demand for expression seems inevitable. The challenge of the mid-life transition for females is, however, the reverse of that for men. For men, what is fundamentally required is an increased receptiveness to the inner world and the development of trust in it. Both these tasks require the overcoming of resistance to this world and the climbing down from the comfortable heights of rationality. Whereas for women, in the main, there does not exist a resistance to the inner world to overcome; rather do women need to overcome a profound sense of inferiority with respect to their knowledge, intellectual abilities and competence in dealing with the outside world. As Emma Jung says:

> With the animus, the emphasis does not lie on mere perception . . . but true to the nature of the logos, the stress is on knowledge and especially on understanding. It is the function of the animus to give meaning rather than the image.

In pragmatic terms the tension that is associated with the emergence of this aspect of women that occurs in the mid-life period is to do with developing a sense of knowledge and accomplishment that belongs exclusively to them in their own right as individuals. This task is an anxiety-provoking one and is rendered additionally difficult by the hostility directed towards women who return to the work force and become successful. In many instances, if they are to be recognized, they have to not just be competent, but extra-competent, simply because they are women. But despite this, in many respects the mid-life crisis seems less traumatic and depressing for women than it does for men, although the start, I believe, is more difficult and frightening since very few women, although hopefully they are increasing in numbers, have thought about life beyond the point of full-time mothering. Models for women who return to the work force are only now, through the direct aegis of the women's movement, becoming visible. To be a woman has for so long been the same as being a wife and mother. The changing social climate towards one of gradually accepting the notion of a female career other than mothering, has provided some guidelines for the future, once the initial nervousness and shock are overcome. As Gail Sheehy says:

> ... women are much more likely to see a realm of unimagined opportunities opening up in the middle years. An initial sense of danger and timidity may give way to invigoration. For most of them there are still so many firsts ahead.

So in many respects the possibilities of resolution for a female are both more visible and acceptable, since her resolution has to do with establishing competence, knowledge and self-respect in the objective outside world; the environment is there and waiting, a path at least mapped. This is so vastly different from the situation for men, who as yet have to carve an identity course beyond that of a full-time occupation and career. Being a woman was, until recently, equated with being a mother, which role terminated with motherhood, leaving a woman free — often alarmingly so — to move into other areas. Being a man is equated with 'careerhood' and socially acceptable alternatives remain hidden and invisible. So on this external basis alone, the crisis is likely to be less difficult for women. In addition women seem, in general, to have less resistance to listening to their inner, subjective world of thought, feelings and experiences. Hence the stimulus for change is often more accessible to them and they have less difficulty in trusting the intuitive than men. Ironically it is this very skill that men need to set as a major goal of the mid-life crisis. For both these reasons the crisis, whilst still being difficult — since all change is — will be less traumatic at the personal level for women than for men.

However at the interpersonal level, in the area of marital interaction, the situation is unlikely to be as smooth, since in her husband's eyes a wife may well come to personify the very situation he seeks. Whilst most of this personification belongs to the realm of fantasy, it can nevertheless be the source of considerable anger, hatred and envy from husbands towards their wives. Once again it is the phenomenon of projection and counter-projection that both characterizes and structures the interaction.

From the women's point of view, however, the husband may appear to have all the attributes and opportunities that she is increasingly becoming aware of. In her eyes he has freedom, freedom from the physical boundaries of a house, freedom from the routine of looking after children and freedom to relate to other people. By the mid-life period many men have experienced some, if not considerable, success and recognition in the outside world, whereas by contrast many wives feel totally and utterly unrecognized. A woman may also perceive her husband as having had a disproportionate opportunity to advance his career by way of education, hard work etc. whereas, again by contrast, she may well feel a failure. Even if a woman has worked during this period when she was bearing and rearing children it was very often part-time work, which does not contribute in any substantial way to her sense of competence. More often than not a woman goes to work in order to assist the family income; that is, she works as part of her mother role, not as an individual. The choice in this situation is frequently imposed upon her, or rather removed, and the work she engages in is not a reflection of an inner choice related to her own psychological needs for growth and development. A nationwide study conducted by the University of Michigan Institute for Social Research in 1969 provides some confirmation of this point, in so far as it ascertained that seven-eighths of all women who worked held jobs in order to 'help make ends meet'. Working in order to help make ends meet tends, emotionally, to be an extension of the mother role and not a separate expression of one's inner pattern. A woman, therefore, may come to see her husband as at least having the freedom to choose his position of employment and further, as having the possibility of a career in which he is interested. This amounts to the feeling that her work is compulsory whilst the husband's is voluntary, in so far as he has a choice. In some situations women simply feel that they have to go to work because their husbands are inadequate providers; such a feeling can generate considerable hostility in the relationship, since it captures and comments closely on the inner struggles of many men.

All of these attitudes are likely to generate some very basic feelings of envy, jealousy, hatred and anger. Many women, as they begin their mid-life passage, may feel that 'men have got it made'. When this anger and resentment is met with an equal if not greater amount from husbands, then it is perfectly understandable that such marriages often go through a very difficult period. Other events can often serve as foci for these feelings, and inhibit a deeper understanding of the process. For example, extra-marital affairs are not uncommon as an expression of the male mid-life crisis. They can have a complex set of motivations but in essence they have to do with a man's need to rebel, express freedom in reaction to the felt absence of it, plus the need to be reassured of his physical attractiveness in the face of increasing age. At another level, as we will discuss later, an affair can be initiated and sustained by a man's inner awakening of his repressed side, which tends to be his feelings. This can lead him into a succession of affairs which are an external manifestation of the inner disturbance of his own feminine aspects. In this case it is the 'inner' woman he is pursuing, his anima, not the external one.

However regardless of the motivation, extra-marital liaisons on the husband's part can serve as the focus for a woman's accumulated sense of resentment at her absence of freedom and opportunities for expressing herself. In addition they can confirm her already existing sense of loss of physical attractiveness, which, to a woman going through her mid-life crisis, would be an especially sensitive issue. So often does an affair encapsulate, for both partners, all the features of a mid-life crisis, that it is not suprising that it should generate, even in couples who at least are intellectually committed to such freedom, an enormous and disproportionate amount of negative feeling.

For the male, his wife's reaction frequently serves as the needed emotional confirmation and justification for his belief that he has married the wrong woman and further, that he is entitled to his freedom: 'After all', he may well tell himself, 'I have supported them all these years'. With some men, in addition to reaffirming their waning sense of youthful masculinity an affair can have the quality of being 'deserved', the freedom it represents being seen as a sort of repayment for services rendered to the family. For other men it simply has the quality of a hostile adolescent rebellion and a stubborn refusal to conform to external rules and mores any longer. Finally for some men, this rebellion and affair provide the necessary impetus for them to bring about a termination of the marriage. The mid-life period can often simply provide an appropriate opportunity to leave a marriage that has long since ceased to function satisfactorily. An affair, in this case, merely represents the end of a long process of separation and divorce, *not* the beginning, despite the attempts of the aggrieved party to see it as the beginning and the cause of the break-up. When all these feelings converge with the deep-felt confusion that men experience in the mid-life period, an extremely negative and destructive marital interaction can ensue. This is because the man is inclined to project all his resentments, frustrations, anxieties, fears, etc. onto his wife. She may well become in his eyes an all-bad and negative object, whereas the mistress by contrast may carry the image of a pure angel, untarnished by the vicissitudes of life — in short, is the 'perfect woman'. Just as women tend to feel 'men have it made', the husbands tend to feel the reverse, and perceive their wives as having all the freedoms, none of the harsh competition and performance anxiety of the male world and none of the meaninglessness of an unsatisfying job. In short, what is likely to occur in a marriage in the early and middle phases of this mid-life transition is that each partner sees the other as having those things which he or she feels deprived of.

The paradox of such projections is that they both make possible resolution, yet at the same time can render it impossible. Which direction the process will take is partly determined by the pattern of communication and problem-solving strategies that couples have utilized in the past. If a commitment to openness has characterized the relationship, a willingness to at least share the burden of the struggle to form and sustain an alive relationship, then in all probability the projections will provide the first clue as to what is wrong within oneself. What we project onto others, or, in this instance, what men project onto their wives, is equivalent to an explicit statement of the implicit and previously unrecognized inner dilemmas. Hence their externalization makes possible recognition and ultimately re-ownership of one's qualities, needs or whatever. However such a process requires a high degree of integrity, honesty and a commitment to personal growth despite, and indeed because of, the costs. The more likely reaction is that the projections will not be seen as externalizations of one's own inner conflicts but will simply be seen as 'really' existing out there in one's partner. The mid-life transition in these marriages can be traumatic, violent and predominantly destructive with regression to more immature patterns of behaviour, rather than any progression towards individual growth. From amongst these marriages, which are characterized by projection and a refusal to see and to own what belongs to oneself, comes a sizeable proportion of those marriages ending in legal divorce. These are the marriages in which an outer divorce, an actual divorce, is obviously less costly emotionally and indeed, is perhaps more appropriate, than the inner divorce spoken of previously. In yet other marriages the mid-life transition is responded to by a burying of one's head in the sand, so to speak. It is seen as a period to go through and put up with, but not as an opportunity for growth. The psychic energy that is tied up in maintaining the projections is then not available for growth, and the marriage, after a short period of turbulence, a nervous flicker, usually returns to a stable, devitalized, safe, boring state.

If, however, the challenge is accepted then the marriage can undergo a substantial change and a renewed reason for being married can evolve. This change is very often characterized by a more flexible definition of roles, with males taking on more of what is traditionally seen as 'female' and females taking up employment of their choice, retraining, or seeking further education where appropriate. Such changes do not occur overnight and demand an experimental attitude on the couple's part, a capacity to ask 'What sort of marriage do we want for ourselves?'. Implicit in this question is a partial, if not full, rejection of the traditional views of marriage: it represents a drawing away from collective definitions and a moving towards an individual one. However this process, this movement, does not have the luxury of standardized guidelines, and hence a prolonged period of uncertainty and confusion is inevitable. Partners moving at a different pace, as already mentioned, can be a source of tension and may generate considerable self-doubt. A natural response to this self-doubt is to rush back to old methods and definitions, or alternatively, to seek instant, trendy, pre-packaged solutions external to oneself. Hence a spontaneous rush into a commune can prove to be a disastrous choice if it represents a panic reaction and an escape from the struggle of working out the right mix for oneself.

Other factors that can inhibit the process of resolution have to do with what one could call points of painful coincidence or similarity. For example, one man I interviewed had decided to 'drop out of the rat race', in short to refuse a promotion and the necessary extra involvement in work that it demanded, so as to be able to accept an increased involvement with his family. Whilst part of him was very comfortable with this choice it became an increasingly difficult choice to maintain as his wife had returned to the workforce and was rapidly earning promotion and recognition. His wife's success reawakened in him some unresolved feelings about success and competence and generated some envy. Whilst this did not result in him surreptitiously undermining his wife, he was honest enough to admit that he felt like doing this, since his wife's success somehow symbolized what he felt was his failure. Perhaps it *was* his failure, perhaps not, but either way a change in the status quo, or the *modus operandi*, of a relationship will generate tension, particularly when that change involves redefinition of established male and female roles. Although this is not the place to expand on it, quite clearly, marriages in which both partners are in occupations they enjoy raises considerable issues such as who's entitled to live where and to take what promotion. Again one may expect that an ability to handle such issues would be one of the consequences of change, if a couple have decided that a dual-career marriage is their individual way.

In fact this last phase is the critical one and provides the basis for concluding the discussion on marriage and the mid-life crisis. To go on *ad nauseam* about the ways in which couples may change, to provide a sort of shopping list of helpful alternatives, would be foreign to the spirit of this book and the journey of the mid-life. If one single message emerged from my interviews, it was that marriage can provide the crucible within which the necessary change or transformation can occur. However it is imperative that this change is initiated and finds its roots in the individual psyche. If nothing else, what the mid-life transition can provide for both partners of a marriage is a safe environment within which they can take some tentative steps towards creating and discovering this personal sense of purpose and meaning. The essential characteristics are a capacity to allow the space within which the experiment can begin and a willingness not to dismiss one's partner's request to try something as 'silly'. On the contrary, thoughts, dreams, feelings expressed tentatively and often with fear of rejection, should be seen as the early stumbling steps of an adult psychological toddler; the first steps towards actively unfolding the inner blueprint. The process and the manifestation of the blueprint will be different for each individual, but the effects of thwarting it will be identical: namely, the continuation of each partner's feelings of resentment, meaninglessness and emptiness, and the sense of spending one's life marching to another drummer's tune.

7 Summary and overview of the crisis

We have now viewed the mid-life crisis through the eyes of the poets, the lives of Fechner, Freud and Jung, and have explored the inner and outer ramifications of the crisis in a man's everyday life. Particular attention was paid to the manifestations of the crisis in a man's personal and occupational life.

Several major themes characterized these discussions commencing with the idea that the mid-life crisis could be a 'creative illness'. Other themes included the loss of identity and the struggle to restructure or reconstruct an old hero, and to create a new hero, a new vision, a new *raison d'être*. A parallel theme was that of grief and mourning for the loss of youth and its associated ambitions, dreams and sense of eternal possibility. Intrinsically related to mourning was the issue of accepting and realizing one's own mortality, and of forsaking one's fantasies of immortality and omnipotence.

Implicit throughout the entire discussion has been the assumption that this period of transition, this crisis, is inevitable and unavoidable. This is not to say that individuals do not develop a variety of strategies for avoiding and denying its existence. But the active denial of a phenomenon ought not to be equated with its non-existence. In simple terms this crisis could be seen as being as inevitable as the passing of years, and as bringing with it a new and alternative task for the second half of life. This alternative task was seen as consisting of the development of previously ignored or sacrificed aspects of self, aspects that had been suppressed in order to achieve the goals of the first half of life. In a man's case these goals are, traditionally, to do with mastery and achievement in the outside world. Hence the task for most men in western society is to do with the development of the inner aspects of their being, the aspects of feeling, intuition and fantasy: in short, those aspects which correlate with a creative life, in which a man is guided by his own inner purpose and not the distractions of the external world. Søren Kierkegaard puts this eloquently, albeit in a somewhat antiquated style when he declares, 'To will to be himself is a man's true vocation'. To Kierkegaard 'self' is related to consciousness, and hence the more man is aware of himself the more conscious he is, or in Kierkegaard's words, 'the more self'. For our purposes, increased consciousness can be seen as deriving from a desire to allow awareness of, and give expression to, the inner aspects of our being, both negative and positive, that have laid dormant in the first half of life.

However this inner urge for expression that often manifests itself in the early stages as doubt, is experienced as a crisis, since it disturbs the existing homeostasis. Thus although one can agree wholeheartedly with Kierkegaard's dictum that 'To will to be himself is a man's true vocation', it is equally true that this is an anxiety-provoking vocation: the early stages of questioning are marked by a profound sense of meaninglessness and often accompanied by inner turmoil. The way in which a man perceives this crisis would seem to be determined by a multitude of factors, amongst which are disposition, family interaction and marriage. However it seems reasonably clear that three board categories or types of response exist. These are for a man to perceive this crisis, this disturbance to his homeostasis, as a threat, as a loss, or as a challenge.

If a man perceives it as a threat — and one suspects that the man who is orientated towards the physical, materialistic, outside world is most likely to do so — then his behaviour is equally likely to follow a recognizable pattern. This pattern will be characterized by a desire to 'get on top of it', to ward off with frantic activity the impending and ominous sense of inner despair and disquiet. One man I interviewed had re-defined his purpose as being to undertake even more physical exercise, only this time in the form of marathon running! This was a man whose considerable success in the business world had come from his irrepressible drive for superiority. This in turn was related to his feeling of being grossly undervalued in his family of origin. His father, mother and brother were all academically gifted and he had been allocated the role of the unintelligent member of the family. This, coupled with his very inadequate physique as an adolescent, had combined to create in him an exceedingly strong drive to succeed, a drive that now made it difficult for him not to perceive the mid-life period as a threat. His reaction was, characteristically, 'I can beat this'. Men of this type who perceive the crisis as a threat, live in fear of failure and not winning prestige and status. Buddhists of the Mahayana sect would describe such men as being in the naive stage of human consciousness. The consciousness of such a man is considered to be exceedingly narrow and bounded by biological desires. Hence he is likely to react to the threat by more of the same behaviour, that is a drive for more power, more status, more possessions and increased physical prowess. All of this is undertaken in the form of frantic activity to drown out the inner noises of discontent.

To perceive the crisis as a loss is more likely to be the response of those men whose orientation toward the world is more emotional and humanitarian. Hence those men who find their way into the helping professions — medicine, teaching, social work etc. — predominate in this category. The next largest proportion in this group is made up of those men in the creative fields of art, music etc. For both these groups of men ideals and grand visions have often been the source of their motivation. The 'great work', the 'great discovery', the 'great contribution': these are the sort of inner images that have moved them. The mid-life period brings into focus the extent to which the hero has been successful, and the meaning of whatever success has been achieved. Alternatively if the dream, the vision, has not been achieved, this period heralds the time of assessing the possibilities of it yet being fulfilled. So for these men, who have an awareness of their inner aspects, there can be an acute sense of loss and despair — a sense of having failed to achieve what is of paramount importance to them, which very often is related to goals of self-development rather than to status, power and other external goals. The characteristic reaction to loss, as we have already seen, is depression and grief. These then are the men who respond to the crisis with despair, for the old hero is dead and no acceptable new hero is forthcoming. Their feeling is predominantly one of depression accompanied by thoughts of suicide with periodic outbursts of rage and anger directed toward those held responsible for the despair.

Tolstoy's hero in *Memoirs of a Madman,* who is troubled in middle age by the idea of death and the meaninglessness of life, provides us with a graphic description of the feelings of these men who experience the crisis as a loss:

> What is life for? To die? To kill myself at once? No, I am afraid. To wait for death till it comes? I fear that even more. Then I must live. But what for? In order to die? And I could not escape from that circle. I took up the book, read and forgot myself for a moment, but then again, the same question and same horror. I lay down and closed my eyes. It was worse still.

If the sense of loss and despair continues, then the accompanying depression can serve as a barrier to resolution. For some men it is possible that they choose to continue to perceive the crisis as a loss, since it facilitates an avoidance of the task of reconstructing a new vision and renewing the purpose for being alive. Such a man is called by the Buddhists the 'man of ordinary intellect'. He is seen as having gained some control over his instincts but his psyche is still dominated by the conscious ego. Hence he is inclined to take the good and reject the bad, allocating it to the realm of his unconscious mind and then projecting it onto the outside world. For a man at this stage the Buddhists' advice is 'to recognise, both within and without oneself the working of the law of opposites'. Thus the vital task for these men is to be able to see, and accept, that their persistent complaints about others preventing them from doing this, or being that, is a projection and that indeed, the only person preventing them is themselves. But such a recognition requires, as the Buddhists advise, the ability to see that the opposites, good and bad, are within oneself.

The third way of reacting to the crisis is to see it as a challenge. Jung is an example *par excellence* of this type of response. To see the mid-life crisis as a challenge is to experience it as a creative crisis. The men whose response falls into this category are those who are able to accept, and indeed in many instances initiate, the death of their hero (the necessity of which was revealed to Jung in his dream of Siegfried). As Ellenberger says: 'The subject emerges from this ordeal with a permanent transformation in his personality'. This transformation, as we have discussed, follows a period of intense self-exploration and isolation, taking the form of self-therapy and culminating in a renewed sense of purpose, a new hero. Bearing this in mind it seems plausible to suggest that the mid-life crisis can be a form of the initiatory illness that ancient medicine men or shamans have been described as undergoing. If this be so, then it is possible that it is a period when males can undergo an initiation into true adulthood. We have already discussed how for most men, the values that they operate by, the reasons they hold for being alive, are those which were developed and learnt during their adolescence, and are mostly to do with success, a career etc. With the majority of men it is only with the emergence of the mid-life period that these values come to be questioned. That is, the early to middle part of one's adulthood, as a male, is lived in accordance with an adolescent world view. Thus the mid-life crisis could be seen as an opportunity for initiation out of adolescence into adulthood. This suggestion gains added credence when one reflects on the self-healing qualities of the initiatory illness of neophyte shamans and the renewed sense of purpose with which they emerge from the illness. Both these qualities, as we have already seen, are characteristic of a creative-illness-type mid-life crisis. Further support can be derived by examining the nature of the initiation process itself. According to Mircea Eliade:

> We know that, during their initiatory dreams, future shamans witness their own dismemberment by 'spirits' or 'demons' who play the role of masters of initiation ... In short we are dealing with ecstatic experiences whose structure is initiatory — a symbolic death is followed by renewal of the candidate's organs and his resurrection.

This passage, if taken symbolically, could be seen as being about the killing of the hero of one's youth, followed by a renewal process — both of which I have consistently argued to be necessary to a successful resolution of the mid-life crisis. In this sense then one can see the initiatory illness, the coming to some understanding and awareness of the inner forces that move us (the 'spirits' or 'demons'), as a process which results in self-healing and renewed purpose — as was so evidently the case with Fechner, Freud and Jung. By undergoing this initiation we can free ourselves from the bonds of adolescence and the chains of the hero of our youth, and come to a deeper and intrinsically self-healing understanding of ourselves. Perhaps the mid-life crisis offers us the challenge of becoming our own shaman! It may well achieve this result if it is perceived as a challenge, a challenge to develop and explore the previously ignored aspects of ourselves. As T.S. Eliot says in *Little Gidding:*

> We shall not cease from exploration
> And the end of all our exploring
> Will be to arrive where we started
> And know the place for the first time.

8 The Self and the anima

Throughout the discussion so far, which has primarily concentrated on a description or study of the mid-life crisis, several ideas, themes, or concepts have been alluded to. The *leitmotiv,* or representative theme, has been the need to facilitate and encourage the development of an accepting reflective attitude towards one's inner world. Implicit and often explicit throughout the discussion has been the assertion that the second half of life heralds the death of the old hero, the existing *raison d'etre* or purpose in life, and brings with it the demand for attention to the inner world. The tasks, achievements and successes of the first half of life are invariably and by necessity to be found in the outside world; however in going about these tasks, in pursuing these heroes, other aspects of an individual have to be sacrificed and their development and expression forfeited. In our western society it is a male's inner world of feeling, fantasy, and capacity for relationships — in short the eros principle — which is sacrificed and relegated to the back room so to speak. In psychological terms the 'back room' is the unconscious mind, that part of our psyche about which we have no conscious awareness or knowledge. Hence those aspects of self which are forfeited or sacrificed in order to achieve the external goals of the first half of life, are not lost forever or killed, but merely relocated, in our unconscious inner world.

Taking, then, the demand of the second half of life to be the redemption, the reawakening and cultivation of this inner world, culminating in its integration with the outer world: how does one proceed to meet this demand? Or in terms of the ideas presented in the previous chapter, how does one develop one's own inner shamanistic abilities? In short, how does an individual become his own shaman? How do we bring forth the self-healing qualities which enable us to emerge from the mid-life crisis? The challenge of answering these questions will be the task of the remainder of this book.

Whilst it would be attractive to offer neat, tidy, prepackaged solutions, the attraction would be derived from the childish quality of such simplistic solutions, which hold the promise of rescuing us from our sense of despair. Regrettably the rescuing would be temporary, a form of distraction, which would serve to inhibit the very real work that needs to be undertaken if any movement towards inner completion is to occur. As Jung so poignantly states:

> The serious problems of life, however, are never fully solved. If ever they should appear to be so, it is a sure sign that something has been lost. The meaning and purpose of a problem seem to lie not in its solution, but in our working at it incessantly.

The remainder of this book will be concerned with the 'working at it', of which the first step must be to increase our understanding of the phenomenon itself. In an analogous sense one can say that the symptoms have been described and it is now necessary to make a diagnosis, leading to the prescription of some treatment strategies.

Any diagnosis, regardless of the field of endeavour in which it is made, involves some form of theory or theoretical thinking. For example, the diagnosis of an engine fault requires an understanding of mechanical and often electrical theory. Theory and theoretical thinking are the internal models we construct of the world. Hence theory ought not be considered or evaluated in simplistic terms of whether it is true or false, but rather in terms of whether it is useful or not in helping us to understand the events or phenomena we are confronted with. Thus psychological theory is concerned with providing models about the inner world of man and his psyche. I make this claim despite the fact that in recent time psychology has reneged on this task and sought consolation in the more simplistic outer-world reality of behaviourism or man's overt behaviour. However in terms of the phenomena with which this book is concerned it is the models and theories of the inner world that are undoubtedly of most use to us. Further, it should be obvious by now that I regard one man's theories, namely those of C.G. Jung, as being particularly useful. This is not meant to imply that other theories are not valid or valuable, rather that the theories of Jung have made most sense to me in my attempts to unravel the phenomenon of the mid-life crisis. His theories, unlike other theories such as those of Sigmund Freud or Melanie Klein, are almost exclusively concerned with the second half of life and hence in this sense are the most appropriate.

We have already alluded to Jung and Jungian theory, firstly in focussing on his own mid-life transition, and secondly in using such ideas as anima, animus and individuation. Given Jung's own struggle with the mid-life period and in particular the development of his self-healing capacity through self-exploration and analysis, it seems entirely appropriate to draw on his theory for the present discussion. I hope those readers who are familiar with the works of Jung will forgive me for the overly simplistic discussion and for the inevitable omissions that will occur. My justification for taking this approach is that this is not a text on Jungian theory but rather a book concerned with men in the mid-life period, for which aspects of Jungian theory are an invaluable aid to understanding.

For those readers who wish to explore Jung's theory in greater detail I would recommend the one book in which he wrote directly for the lay reader, *Man and his Symbols,* edited and conceived by C.G. Jung, plus his autobiography *Memories, Dreams, Reflections.* As anyone attempting to read Jung will very quickly discover, his theoretical writings are discursive and esoteric, which has undoubtedly contributed to the general ignorance of, and on occasions, prejudice against, Jungian theory when compared to the works of Sigmund Freud.

Because Jung's theoretical thinking is so wide ranging and extensive it is difficult to ascertain an appropriate starting point without doing violation to the richness of his views. However of all his concepts, that of individuation is both central to his thinking and at the same time can be considered as providing a definition of the goal of development as conceived by Jung. In Jung's own words individuation 'denotes the process by which a person becomes a psychological individual, that is a separate indivisible unity or whole'. For Jung the supreme state, the goal towards which an individual's development is headed, is wholeness, and individuation is the term he uses to describe this inner journey towards wholeness. An equivalent of this process and journey can be found in Bunyan's *Pilgrim's Progress*. A few more or less equivalent terms for the individuation process are 'the search for individual identity', 'the search for authenticity', 'self-actualization', all of which refer to this seemingly innate disposition to move towards a sense of completion and wholeness. Individuation can be seen as describing psychic growth, inevitable growth, towards an integration of the world of consciousness, the outer world, and the inner world of the unconscious. It is important to distinguish this profound process of individuation from the more immature and superficial external display of difference, which we would normally call individualism. The process of individuation is the age-old process of the inner journey, the unfolding of self, the becoming what it is that we intrinsically are; thus individuation can be seen as the western equivalent of the eastern process of self-realization.

The phrase 'the unfolding of self' captures the essential qualities of the relationship between the Self and individuation, since the Self is the goal or final point of individuation. It can be seen as being the common midpoint through which the conscious and unconscious pass, and the integration of these two aspects through the process of individuation results in a shift of the psychic centre of gravity from the ego, or conscious world, to the midpoint, or centre of the psyche, the Self. This in Jungian terms results in a major transformation of the personality, the type of metamorphosis we have already witnessed in Jung himself, as he emerged from the mid-life period. In essence it is a shift from an ego-centred 'I' base to a non-personal, or more cosmic, central position, the Self. Indeed Jung defines the Self as follows:

> The Self is not only the centre but also the whole circumference which embraces both consciousness and unconscious; it is the centre of this totality, just as the ego is the centre of the conscious mind.

Marie-Louise von Franz also speaks of this 'centre' quality:

> The goal of individuation, as pictured in unconscious images, represents a kind of midpoint or centre in which the supreme value and the greatest life-intensity are concentrated. It cannot be distinguished from the images of the supreme value of the various religions.

Perhaps another way of expressing this is to say that the goal of individuation is wholeness, and wholeness is related to the experience of the highest end, the awareness of Self, the conjunction of Atman and Brahman. Marie-Louise von Franz takes this suggestion a little further when she says: 'The experience of the Self brings a feeling of standing on solid ground inside oneself, on a patch of inner eternity which even physical death cannot touch'. It is, as Jung says, the process by which 'every living thing becomes what it was destined to become from the beginning'.

This discussion of individuation has introduced the ideas of reconciling opposites and integrating the conscious and unconscious. However, before we discuss these in detail it is important to point out that the relevance of individuation to the mid-life crisis is that, in the broadest sense, it is the process that commences in earnest in the second half of life. This is not to say that it is not operative in the first half, since clearly it is, but it is in the second half of life that Jung would claim that, if we are to reach an inner sense of serenity and harmony, we must rediscover those neglected aspects that we have removed to the 'back room'. The first half of the individuation process can be seen as being concerned with the development of our main psychological characteristics, being our 'superior functions', in Jungian terms. So, for example, if a man was predominantly an intellectual type, then individuation in the first half of life would be concerned with differentiation and development of this function. Individuation in the first half is concerned with consolidation of our conscious personality, which can more precisely be termed the consolidation of the ego, the personality mechanism by which we adapt to the outer world. The reason why individuation commences in earnest in the second half is because the psyche, in Jungian terms, has a type of compensatory mechanism that creates — during the period of mid-life crisis — the demand to redress the imbalance and develop the neglected aspects of one's psyche. Hence for the intellectual man the need is often to develop his feeling side, his compassionate and caring qualities. It is the eruption of this inevitable inner demand for balance and integration that lies behind the malaise and sense of purposelessness that men express in mid-life.

In short the archetypal hero of the first half which presents the ideals of power, success, technical competence and other outer world or ego values, dies or becomes incapable of providing a meaningful purpose, leaving one in a state of confusion regarding the task of the second half. This task can be succinctly summed up as cultivating the symbolic life and the reflective attitude, as, in essence, developing the inner world. This is a necessary part of integration and the movement towards wholeness. This means creating an alternative 'hero' so to speak, or heroic attitude, that encompasses the goal of reflection and inner development.

As has so often been mentioned, the individuation process has a quality of inevitability about it and indeed, it could be said that to be human is to be part of the individuation process and that the two are inseparable. This urge, or imperative, to unfold, seems no less able to be retarded or stopped in human beings than it does in the animal or plant kingdom. As Emma Jung says: 'The urge toward increased consciousness seemingly proceeds from the archetypes, as though so to speak, there were an instinct tending toward this goal'. I believe that this urge is certainly instinctual, and further, can be seen as being related to the archetypes. This term brings us to two further aspects of Jung's theory —

archetypes and archetypal images — which we shall briefly discuss, since an understanding of them is critical to developing a deeper understanding of the mid-life crisis.

In the simplest possible terms it can be said that for Jung human beings have a personal unconscious which primarily contains the products of their day-to-day interactions that have in the main been pushed out of their conscious mind, or repressed, in the technical sense. However, according to Jung, in addition to this personal aspect of our psyche we also have a transpersonal, or universal aspect, which is derived not from our personal everyday lives but from the fact that we are human beings. It is a form of universal unconscious, which Jung terms the collective unconscious, and it is this part of our psyche that connects us to our ancestral past as a species, not as an individual. As Jung says: 'The collective unconscious contains the whole spiritual heritage of mankind's evolution born anew in the brain structure of every individual'. In a sense the collective unconscious contains the deposits of the 'experience of being human'. In this layer of the psyche are to be found the archetypes. These are the inborn potential, or instinctual predispositions, or more simply, the instinctual patterns for reacting in certain ways to particular universal situations. They are, if you like, the equivalent of such instinctual behaviour patterns in the bird kingdom as migratory habits. In other words archetypes are patterns of psychological instinctual behaviour, predispositions to behave in specific ways. Because some processes — for instance life, death, mothering, growing old etc. — are generic to the human situation, the collective unconscious, in the form of archetypes, contains the instinctual patterns of response to these situations.

However this is not to say, as Jung so very often pointed out, that therefore we all, regardless of race or culture, react in the same way. Not at all. Rather does it mean we all have inherited, as part of the human evolution, predispositions to respond in certain ways. How we manifest this inner potential will vary from culture to culture and individual to individual. The nearest analogy I can think of is that hunger is a universal instinct but how we go about expressing it varies enormously and is determined by our individual disposition, as by our environment and culture with which we interact. Another way of expressing this fairly abstruse concept, a concept that can be regarded as one of Jung's major contributions, is to think of the archetypes as sort of psyche moulds or casts into which we pour our unique aspects, culminating in what has been termed an archetypal image. The collective unconscious contains several archetypes that are imperceptible but which actualize themselves as inner images. That is, they exist in form only and gain substance as an image. E.A. Bennett gives a very succinct and clear definition of an archetype:

> The archetypes represent all the general human situations; any universally human mode of behaviour is an archetype. Inevitably these have taken innumerable forms and they become perceptible as images in the mind.

It is these archetypal images that move us, that give meaning and purpose to our lives, but over which we have limited, if any, control. These are centres and fields of force that emerge and cannot be consciously willed into action, but which influence our attitudes and behaviour toward such universal events as birth and death.

It is this emergent, instinctual quality that contributes to and largely determines the inevitability of the individuation process, since one can say that this process itself is an archetypal process; we do not choose it or will it, we *are* it, and the governing and directing overseer of its unfoldment is the Self. It is as if we are destined to complete ourselves, as if the soul has a homing instinct, and the Self is both the regulator and goal of this completion or individuation process. The archetypes are in one sense negatives that await development, or pieces of a jigsaw which when properly related to each other form the whole. However unlike the jigsaw, it seems as if a quite specific timing mechanism operates in the collective unconscious, not dissimilar to the time-releasing mechanisms of physical instincts such as walking, sitting etc. in infants, whereby the development of certain archetypes takes place as appropriate, at certain critical stages.

The Self archetype is the prime mover, but in the process of moving towards this central point of integration, certain other aspects of being, other instinctual patterns, have to be fulfilled and integrated. The major one that is of concern to us is the anima archetype, since it is the release or emergence of this archetype that appears to occur in a man's life between the ages of 35 and 45. Whilst some readers may object to the idea of certain psychological factors in the form of archetypes demanding expression and fulfilment at age-specific stages, might I remind them that such ideas are readily accepted with respect to children and child development. The scholarly work of Piaget attests to the validity of this statement. The interesting question is why we find it difficult to accept that such stage-specific developmental tasks should not continue on throughout our adult lives rather than be confined to childhood? It is this idea of such specific inner demands for growth, within the broad conception of a general instinct towards completion, that I believe makes most sense of the male mid-life crisis.

It is the anima archetype that is the critical one for a man as he enters the second half of his life, so we now need to discuss this in some detail. The most comprehensive, although by no means clearest, definition of the anima, which is Latin for 'soul image', is given by Jung himself:

> Every man carries within him the eternal images of woman, not the image of this or that particular woman, but a definite feminine image. This image is fundamentally unconscious, an hereditary factor of primordial origin engraved in the living organic system of man, an imprint or 'archetype' of all the ancestral experiences of the female, a deposit, as it were, of all the impressions ever made by women — in short, an inherited system of psychic adaptation... I have called this image the 'Anima'.

In short the anima refers to the feminine aspects of a man, the 'unconscious woman'; it becomes literally the container of all those feminine personality-components of man that have been repressed and removed into the personal unconscious. The mould of this archetype is feminine and it is given actuality in a man's everyday life by attracting to it and attaching itself to those feminine, repressed aspects of males; it is both personal and transpersonal.

We have repeatedly discussed the idea that in achieving the goals of the first half of his life the typical man represses and leaves underdeveloped certain aspects of himself. Those features which are developed in the first half of life are what have socially come to be regarded as masculine traits, whilst those which are underdeveloped and repressed at an early age are traits normally associated with feminine qualities. The first half of a man's life tends to witness the development of attributes governed by the logos principle, such attributes as rational thought, logic, technical and instrumental mastery, power, prestige: in general, man's ego-conscious attributes. What this leaves underdeveloped and very often in an infantile state, is the entire realm of feelings, fantasies and capacity for relationships: in general, those attributes for which the governing principle is eros. In this sense we can see how, simply through social conditioning and the adherence to rigid role definitions, we have come to regard some aspects of our nature as masculine and some as feminine. However within the framework of a Jungian perspective one has both these aspects within oneself, and a very basic and central part of the individuation process is the integration of these opposites within the one individual. This is the 'inner marriage' that we have already discussed in relation to marriage and the mid-life crisis.

There does exist, as Anthony Storr mentions in relation to definitions of the anima, 'a multiplicity of ill-formed definitions of the same thing', which adds to the difficulty of discussing and understanding the anima archetype. One way to proceed is to give careful attention to the fact that it is both an archetype, and thus part of the deep layers of the collective unconscious, and at the same time part of a male's personal unconscious. By grasping this one can then come to the broader view that the anima is the realm of fantasy and the way in which a man relates to his own unconscious. The anima is predominantly conditioned by eros, that is, by the principles of union and of relationship, and hence it will more often than not be these aspects which are underdeveloped in a male. These are very often the aspects which men label 'irrational' and consider, in a thoroughly prejudicial manner, to be exclusively 'female characteristics'. It is these areas, the areas of fantasy, feeling and the intuitive function that have been repressed into the unconscious in the interest of developing the masculine ego-consciousness, that come to be personified by the anima, the 'woman within'.

Thus to the extent that a man has developed the outer aspects of himself, to that extent his inner world very often lies underdeveloped. To resort to a stereotype, one could say that the high-powered, successful, hard-hitting, no-nonsense business executive is in all probability infantile and peevish, nit-picking and childish in his emotional life. This is the type of man whose wife very often has to carry the full burden of her husband's underdeveloped aspects, since she becomes the focus of his illogical moods, irritating platitudes, and sheer incapacity to form an intimate relationship. These moods are often the first sign of the anima archetype stirring and the consequent inner demand to redress the imbalance. Here the self-regulating psychic mechanism of compensation is saying to the man, 'It is time to attend to developing the inner world since you have paid adequate attention to the outer'. It is as if he is adult on the outside and infantile on the inside, hence the very childish quality of the emotional displays, which for all the world can look like adult temper tantrums! This voice he hears is his anima speaking, and it can be seen as being given voice and impetus by the archetype. Each man's anima manifestation and challenge will vary according to which aspects he has ignored and repressed in pursuing the goals of the first half of life. However the beginnings of this seemingly inevitable process that occurs and brings in the mid-life transition will fairly consistently take the form of inexplicable and often out of character moodiness, irritability and general discontent. The psychological mechanism that usually accompanies this period is that of projection, which we have discussed previously. Within the present context it means a man will tend to take out his moodiness on his wife or female companion, who will be seen as the source of the man's ills. In plain, simple terms she will be blamed for his inner sense of unease and irritability, since she personifies in the outside world the trouble he is experiencing in his inside world from his inner woman, the anima.

It is perhaps a little clearer now why many if not most marriages experience considerable stress around this time. The female literally carries the projection of the man's difficulties in coming to grips with his inner world and his inability to accept these traditionally more feminine aspects of himself. Up until this time in harmonious or working marriages, the female partner has had projected onto her the husband's positive female images, and a man has not had to develop a relationship with the female aspects within himself. As Jung points out, a man's first meeting with his anima is mostly in the negative and unwelcome form. Thus moodiness and irritability can be taken as a sign that a man ought to concentrate on developing a better relationship with those previously neglected aspects of himself. However, so long as he projects these difficulties onto his female partner, they will not be recognized as coming from within himself; hence the first vital step is to stop and listen to what one is actually saying about oneself! Marriage is a difficult place to do this, yet paradoxically it is an appropriate place; but the natural tendency is for the female partner to experience the negative projections as a personal attack and hence she frequently counter-attacks. Such a response serves to reinforce the man's view that he was 'right after all', and projections may come to characterize the relationship, resulting in an inexorable sense of bitterness. This situation is largely brought about by the man's difficulties with his 'inner woman', his irrational, feeling and fantasy aspects, whom his 'outer man', his masculine aspects, wants to go on discrediting and disowning. Such a failure to own his anima can only lead to a progressive immaturity in a man's feeling and relationship aspects, leading, in turn, to an increasingly sterile marriage.

In addition to this obviously negative and potentially destructive outcome of a man's struggle with his anima, another pattern of expression exists which more clearly features the eros principle. In this role the anima personifies the unconscious and is seen to have such characteristics as magic, mystery, fascination, intrigue and knowledge of deep secrets; in other words, to be the French *femme fatale*. Here the man projects all of these qualities, the deep mystery of his own unconscious, onto a female in the outer world. This is the woman the poets so often speak of, the eternal seductress, the ever-alluring mystical female. Keats provides a classic example in his poem *La Belle Dame Sans Merci*:

> I met a lady in the meads
> Full beautiful, a faery's child,
> Her hair was long, her foot was light,
> And her eyes were wild.

Equally is she Helen of Troy or Cleopatra. Jung frequently cites two novels as containing examples *par excellence* of the anima. These are Rider Haggard's *She* and Benoit's *Atlantide*. The theme in both centres around the semi-immortal figure of the mysterious woman. 'She', in Rider Haggard's novel, is, in addition to being spectacularly beautiful, an immortal priestess with a remarkable grasp of the esoteric. Herman Hesse provides a contemporary fiction example in his novel *Steppenwolf*. Here the main character is a withdrawn, alienated man who meets a quiet, ordinary, young woman who seduces him and becomes his initiator into an awareness of who he himself is. Here the attributes of superior and esoteric knowledge, alongside erotic fascination, are the major characteristics of the female. Again one can see these attributes as being a man's projection of the 'inner woman', his anima, that personification of his own feminine psychological tendencies which, in being repressed, remain a mystery to him and hold persuasive fascination.

Such projections can be the compelling force behind an extra-marital affair or series of liaisons. These represent the man splitting these aspects off from himself and projecting them onto a female who he then literally 'falls in love' with. The classic 1930 film entitled *The Blue Angel*, where a straight-laced professor becomes infatuated with a cabaret singer resulting in him finally being a buffoon in her cabaret act, is a fine example of this process at work. As a result of developing his intellectual side, the professor's emotional development has been retarded; hence his childish level of infatuation which reflects the immaturity of his feelings.

The dynamics of this situation are, of course, as previously mentioned, found in many extra-marital affairs. Men will fall head over heels in 'love', swear on a thousand Bibles that this is *the* woman of their life, that this is 'True Love', or assure all and sundry that they are 'meant for each other', that they 'have known each other in a previous life'. On and on go the excessive claims, and it is by observing these very excesses, that one can suspect that the anima is out of control. By and large such relationships are characterized by projection, and the man weaves endless fantasies around the object of his projection. The woman herself and her identity very often seem incidental and one is reminded of the statement found in the frontispiece of some novels — 'any relationship between the characters in this book and any real persons, living or dead, is purely coincidental'!

This projection of the 'all wonderful', the 'beautiful mystical woman' is frequently accompanied by a negative projection onto a man's wife, so that she carries the negative aspects of the anima, those of the witch, the devouring mother, the predatory female. Hence when this situation occurs the emotional atmosphere is highly charged and the possibility of reason or common sense operating is remote.

Time alone will reveal the nature and future of the relationship. If it is based entirely on projection then within a reasonable period, often six months or so, the projection will begin to crumble and a man will look back in utter amazement at the object of his attachment. In other circumstances the projection may serve the purpose of initiating a more personal relationship, and if both partners are capable of open, honest and often painful sharing, they may well discover other aspects of themselves that facilitate the building of a more permanent, mature relationship.

The outcome of such relationships seems to be governed by the nature of the man's awareness of, and working relationship with, his own anima. If these are poorly developed and have been heavily sacrificed in the pursuit of outer values of power, prestige etc., then there is a strong possibility that a repetitive pattern of affairs will emerge, with each woman being the 'real one'. Alternatively, if, as we discussed in relation to marriage, a man has struggled

104

with developing a working relationship with his inner world, his 'inner woman', then the choice and attraction operating in an affair may well represent a mature choice of partner based on a more mature relationship with his own feminine aspects. Such a choice may result in an acceleration of the growth of these aspects, whereas his existing marriage may have prevented the possibility of this growth.

Two other manifestations of what one may call 'projected anima activity' that seem to be increasingly common in our present age are erotica and the occult. Both of these manifestations are clearly reflected in our present day society: the first in the proliferation of erotic material in the form of films and books, and the second, the occult, in the proliferation of gurus, all professing to be chosen dispensers of the mysterious path to truth. In the context of the present discussion it can be seen that both these phenomena reflect, on a social scale, the projections of individual male animas. That is, they are externalizations, now being exploited for commercial gain, of a man's inner dilemmas and conflicts with the feminine aspects of himself. It is no coincidence that the eruption of both erotica and the occult have arisen together and neither is it by chance alone that they have coincided with the emergence of the women's liberation movement. This movement, as we have discussed earlier, has provided the opportunity for men to examine their own oppression, the oppression of their feminine side, and the tyranny of the rigid masculine role definition. It is clear that the effects of this examination are now being experienced, and that the proliferation of erotica, alongside the occult, are two manifestations of the large-scale projection of the anima or inner woman.

That this is so becomes even clearer when we take into account two psychological factors. The first is projection, the placing outside ourselves of aspects of our inner world that our conscious mind wants to reject. The rational male ego-centred psyche wants to deny acceptance of the inner feminine world and thus it is projected outside and not owned as part of himself. The second factor that substantiates the above claim is that, within the framework of Jungian theory, the emergence of an interest in erotica is regarded as one of the most common and regular forms in which the anima first appears. For example Marie-Louise von Franz declares:

> You can say that the vehicle bringing up the anima is sex and sexual fantasy, which in a man's make-up is very often the way in which the world of Eros first wells up into his consciousness. It first is carried, as it were, by sexual fantasies.

Thus men in the mid-life period can find themselves preoccupied with sexual fantasies; for some men these fantasies become the stimulus for pursuing a range of sexual behaviour encompassing both homosexual and heterosexual interests and relationships. This observation that erotic material can 'open the door to a world of feeling and emotion' as Anthony Storr states, adds an extra reason for the trend amongst men to pursue sexual affairs at this stage of their lives. When we further consider that the anima is governed by the Eros principle of union, not logos, then it becomes more readily understandable why an increase or emergence of an interest in erotica should occur during the mid-life period.

In some respects one can see shades of adolescence in this interest, and indeed, in adolescence and the mid-life period, erotica can serve as a form of orientation into relationships with the opposite sex. The critical difference is that at the mid-life period it is serving as an orientation into relationships with the inner female, the anima. The obvious danger is that a man may miss this distinction and go on pursuing the female on the outside of himself; that is, he mistakes the orientation for the task itself. Within marriages, apart from the conflict that can result over extra-marital liaisons, the emergence of Eros in the erotic form of sexual fantasies can disturb the balance of the marital sex life. A man may, seemingly all of a sudden, begin to request of his wife sexual behaviour that has previously been non-existent between them. This may range from the wearing of erotic lingerie to requests for trying different and irregular positions in intercourse. Whilst these requests can greatly enrich a couple's sex life, their initial impact can be very difficult for the wife to accept. Here is her previously predictable, reliable but safe husband, now suggesting what to her are way-out ideas verging on perversions! Such a situation can engender anxiety in the female partner, resulting in her responding disapprovingly towards her husband, or alternatively becoming very suspicious that he has another lover.

Hence this very tentative beginning within a man to bring into consciousness his anima, the feminine side of his personality, can be seriously misunderstood resulting in it being pushed further back into his personal unconscious, perhaps to find its way out at a later date in such symptoms as impotence, sexual obsessions or the total withdrawal into the world of fantasy. On the other hand, if the couple can communicate with trust and have developed some ability to communicate sexually, the emergence of the erotic fantasies that can accompany the mid-life crisis may well be the very necessary input to enrich a couple's sex life and rescue it from the boredom of sameness. In addition, the bringing up of fantasies into consciousness and accepting of them brings with it the repressed feminine side of a man, and as such represents the beginning of a relationship with that part of himself.

The other contemporary manifestation of the anima can be seen in the upsurge of interest in the occult, as has been mentioned, and in various spiritual and pseudospiritual movements. Because the anima can stand for a personification of the unconscious mind, it may come to be seen as containing dark, hidden mysteries and esoteric truths. The world of the occult and pseudospirituality can then provide a perfect hook for these projections. This possibility is greatly increased if the spiritual leader is female, since just as sexually seductive women can provide one form of anima projection, it is also known that another anima type is the 'medium', a female who is acknowledged to be a seer and attributed with mystical powers.

Men in their thirties and forties not uncommonly begin to experience a reawakening of spiritual questioning. This is perfectly in accord with what has been discussed so far with respect to the anima, since a consistent theme of Jung's was that the anima is *naturaliter religiosa,* the soul is by nature religious. By religious he did not mean anything to do with organized religion, but rather that the anima, or soul image, was in essence spiritual. Thus the inner movement of the anima in the mid-life period can bring with it, in some men, an upsurge of interest in spiritual matters. However, as we have seen with other aspects of the anima, its first appearance will be in the form of a projection, usually upon a real woman. When we take into account Frances Wickes' view that 'the anima is not only the unknown woman in man, she is also the unknown element existent in all women', we can see how the mystery of spiritual matters, particularly in the more sensational form of the occult, could manifest itself readily by way of a projection onto a female spiritual leader or pseudospiritualist. Frances Wickes recognizes this possibility when she says, in relation to the projection of the anima:

> Another way of disposing of the problem of the inner woman is to remove her to the world of pseudospirituality where, from a safe distance, her image may be worshipped.

This form of projection does not always require a female figure as such, since religion and in particular spiritual endeavours have a definitely feminine quality about them — for example one says 'mother church'. Therefore a man will not infrequently seek his feminine side, his anima, in embodiments of the feminine such as mysticism and esoteric eastern practices and systems of belief. This can be particularly so for an over-intellectual man, whose inferior function (in Jungian terms) is the feeling function. The arrival of an acclaimed eastern guru — of which there seems no shortage these days — can witness the compulsive, highly organized, emotionally tight, intellectual man suddenly joining a religious or spiritual movement, giving away all his possessions and uncritically following the leader in a contemporary form of the Pied Piper. This all-masculine male can now be seen wearing feminine-style clothing and talking in gentle, concerned tones of an all-loving, feeling being.

In its dramatic quality, this change parallels the situation of the more erotically-orientated man who falls hopelessly in love. Both men display an uncritical childlike adherence to the target of the projection whether that be a real woman or an embodiment of the female. In both cases the distinguishing characteristics are the uncontaminated purity of the object, the all-good, all-wonderful quality, and the male's inability to exercise any critical faculties. The sudden and dramatic quality of these happenings is further evidence that Lady Anima has taken yet another victim!

It would be easy to misconstrue what I have been saying as an attack on all forms of eastern philosophy and religious practices: furthermore as an attack on various Christian sects such as the Children of God and the more recent Charismatic movement, which also exhibit anima-projection behaviour. Such a conclusion would be invalid since, as I made clear in the section on the Self, I hold to the view that the purpose and goal of life, via the individuation process, is the unfolding of Self, which in traditional terms could be described as soul, or one's own divinity. Rather I am saying that as long as these aspects of the inner world are only experienced as a projection, then a man will not recognize them as part of himself and thereby move towards integrating them. They will remain 'out there' and not within him; hence both his dependence on the object of the projection and the childlike quality of his inner world will be maintained. In short, as evidenced by the blind adherence to the spiritual leader that such a man displays, projections of this nature maintain a man's spirit in an infantile state. Nevertheless, it is important to recognize that projection is the first stage of the anima's awakening (as was mentioned in relation to the erotic) and may well lead a man to a deeper and more profound relationship with this part of himself, with his spirit, which may otherwise have been impossible. However the critical task, as we will discuss in the next chapter, lies in recognizing the projective quality, the placing of the inner world onto the outer, and then struggling with the task of reclaiming and integrating it. As Emma Jung states:

> It is not a question of either surrendering his masculinity completely to the service of Lady Anima or losing her entirely, but only of granting a certain space to the feminine, which is also part of his being.

The seductive aspect of projection is that it absolves us from

109

responsibility and we can maintain the childlike luxury of being passive recipients or followers and see the world as happening to us. To maintain this passive position is to abort the process of individuation itself.

Because the anima is both an archetypal and individual figure, its actual manifestation will vary considerably within each individual man. For one man the inner image may be a dark, sensuous, languid female; for another, an effervescent blonde. Alternatively, it may form as an embodiment of the spirit we have just discussed. So whilst the feminine, the collective aspect, remains the same, the inner image is different for different men. This brings us to a brief exploration of the four fantasy solutions to the mid-life crisis that we discussed earlier in relation to a man's occupation. These were, respectively, the fantasies of being a nurseryman, a farmer, a writer and a helper, each of which can be seen as being reflective of the anima.

One of the attributes of the anima is her earthiness, since females symbolically throughout time have been associated with the earth, in which things are fertilized, grow and are nurtured. The Greek goddess, Demeter, is an example *par excellence*. Hence we use the term 'mother earth'. Thus both the farmer and nurseryman fantasies are clearly symbolic expressions of the anima. Men holding on to these fantasies are experiencing an inner demand to return to the earth, to recover the lost woman within and, consistent with the anima-governing principle, to care and nurture, not master. As an aside one could say that on a broad social level, the present growth of organizations to protect the environment (including the anti-uranium movement), can be seen as indicative of the emergence of the feminine in an attempt to redress the imbalance caused by the dominance of logos and the masculine principle. So, in relation to the individual man, can either of the above fantasies be seen as a call to redress the imbalance in his psyche, to pay attention to his own earth, his own feminine aspects.

The farmer and the nurseryman fantasies are to do with the need to dig down into one's own earth and fertilize, cultivate and nurture the inner world that has previously been left as a desert, blown and eroded by the winds of ambition and power. Earth is a receptive domain, one sinks into the earth, is absorbed by the earth. This characteristic further elaborates at a symbolic level the anima — for the anima, as the feminine aspect of man, possesses this receptivity and absence of prejudice towards the irrational and the inner world of fantasy. The fact that it does have these qualities is, as we will discuss further on, the reason why the anima is the guide or mediator between the unconscious and the conscious minds.

The writer fantasy perhaps needs little further discussion since quite clearly such creative urges are reflective of unconscious stirrings and as such reflect the feminine side of man. It is well known that poets throughout the ages have called upon the assistance of the muses, and have experienced the feminine side of their being, the anima, as a *femme inspiratrice*. Dodds, for example, in discussing Plato's types of 'divine madness' says that Plato's third type was 'possession by the Muses', and that Plato declared such possession to be indispensable to the production of the best poetry. In the beginning of *The Odyssey,* Homer calls upon the Muse when he says: 'He hero of the tale which I beg the Muse to help me tell . . .'. In the Celtic tradition Muses are commonplace. W.B. Yeats, in an appendix to a book edited by him on fairy and folk tales of Ireland, talks of the Leanhaun Shee and says of her:

> This spirit seeks the love of men. Most of the Gaelic
> poets, down to quite recent times, have had a Leanhaun
> Shee, for she gives inspiration to her slaves and is indeed
> the Gaelic muse.

Milton begins his mammoth work, *Paradise Lost,* with an appeal to the Muse, the Goddess of Poetic inspiration:

> Of man's first disobedience, and the fruit
> Of that forbidden tree, whose mortal taste
> Brought death into the world, and all our woe,
> With loss of Eden, till one greater man,
> Restore us, and regain the blissful seat,
> Sing, heav'nly Muse.

Here the anima expresses itself in the divine image of the Muse, and as these few quotations show, it is this feminine aspect that the poet calls on to provide him with inspiration.

The urge that a man may feel coming from the unconscious to write represents the stirring of his feminine side. Initially, most men experiencing this fantasy will believe they can write great creative works — such a feeling parallels the early upsurge of 'falling in love'. Thus the elapsing of time and the recognition of the urge for what it is, ought to occur before a man can make a realistic logos assessment of his abilities in this area.

The final fantasy, that of the helper, was often expressed by the men I interviewed and has also been expressed by other men — often those who have changed their careers during their mid-thirties. This fantasy sometimes manifests itself specifically in the image of wanting 'to be with people', 'to be a social worker' or some similar type of 'helper'. The underlying dynamics of this fantasy can be seen as the Eros principle, with the nurturing care aspect coming to the fore. It represents an anima expression of care and relatedness as opposed to the logos principle of rational thought and discrimination. This fantasy then is a fairly clear manifestation of the female aspect or feminine principle within males, and its appearance during mid-life as an urge to care for others ought to be taken seriously since it, like the other fantasies, represents the first step towards integrating the feminine side of a man's personality.

It is to this task, the process of integration, and the difficulties inherent in such a journey that we now turn since, according to Marie-Louise von Franz:

> Only the painful (but essentially simple) decision to take one's fantasies and feelings seriously can at this stage prevent a complete stagnation of the inner process of individuation, because only in this way can a man discover what this figure means as an inner reality. Thus the anima becomes again what she originally was — the 'woman within', who conveys the vital messages of the Self.

9 Approaching the inner world

A connecting thread throughout this book, whether we have been discussing the poets, famous psychologists, or men in relation to their families, marriage or occupation, has been the need to develop the inner world, to cultivate a reflective as opposed to reactive attitude. This, it has been suggested, is the prime purpose and goal of the second half of life, the serious turning towards the uncovering of Self and the struggle towards a greater sense of purpose, wholeness and completion.

In the previous chapter the anima and its role in the movement towards wholeness was discussed. However the discussion primarily concentrated on two aspects: the early, and usually negative, signs of a man's awakening anima — such as moodiness — and the initial mechanism of expression, projection. The task that now remains is that of elaborating on the positive step of developing a relationship with this elusive inner woman, the task of both recognizing and welcoming into the male consciousness these feminine aspects of being. Initially this involves a further brief discussion of projection since, as I have already indicated in the previous chapter, it is via projection that a man may first come to recognize that these other aspects exist at all, albeit initially he is unlikely to recognize them as part of himself. So far we have only discussed the first stage of projection and, whilst pointing out the inherent dangers of getting stuck at this stage and failing to recognize that outside is inside, the task still remains to elaborate on the process of getting beyond this stage. The essence of this process, which can be regarded as the first essential step to be taken towards wholeness, is the withdrawal of the aspect of oneself which has been projected: in other words the taking back into oneself of those features, faults, or qualities that a person has previously only seen as belonging to another. Inevitably the beginning of this process entails the withdrawing of our criticism of the faults of others — usually those closest to us — and the recognition that such faults are part of oneself, and indeed belong to one. However, as was clearly stated in the previous chapter, withdrawing a projection is, to say the least, likely to be experienced with considerable ambivalence. Whilst the inner archetypal drive will be towards integration and individuation, the ego-conscious drive will be to leave the situation as it is. This is simply because by projecting our faults and other aspects of ourselves that are unacceptable to our conscious image, we can avoid the threat, anxiety and responsibility of accepting the onerous task of maturation. Projection is alluring in that it aids and abets our avoidance of the challenge and threat of inner growth and provides, instead, the comfort of the status quo. So long as we see all the faults as being outside ourselves, then we simply do not consciously feel any compulsion to do anything about them. It is as if in contradiction and opposition to the archetypal force of individuation there exists an equal and opposite force in the form of a conservative impulse or archetype to keep things exactly as they are.

In the interplay of these opposing forces, a man will often feel at the one time the impulse to change and to remain the same. Is it therefore any wonder that the first experience of the stirring of an archetypal force of the anima, provoking a man to change, should be experienced as a conflict? Change is by definition a conflict, since regret, loss and sadness must inevitably accompany the giving up of the old to allow the new to flourish. In the terms of this book the death of the old hero is felt as a profound loss and the accompanying feeling is that of grief. Change means loss, and loss means pain, suffering and grief. Hence it is not surprising that the conservative impulse, the force to maintain the status quo, often emerges superior, since change is a painful, stressful and confusing process. Thus to withdraw a projection, to actually move towards accepting that 'outside' is 'inside', is almost against man's conscious nature, yet paradoxically it is his destiny; as Oscar Wilde said: 'Evolution is the law of life, and there is no evolution except toward individualism'. Further he declared: 'When this tendency is not expressed, it is a case of artificially arrested growth, or of disease or of death'. For Wilde 'individualism' is self-realization and hence identical with the process of individuation. Thus despite, and indeed because of, the conservative impulse, the instinctual urge towards wholeness, of which the first step is to withdraw projections, continues to demand expression.

What is critical yet incredibly difficult to ascertain, is that moment, that point in time, that impetus, that results in initiating the withdrawal. This moment, in the men I talked with, seemed to be characterized by their experiencing the full impact of this inner war between the conservative impulse and the progressive impulse. Somehow they either consciously or semi-consciously experienced doubts about the rightness of their approach to the world or way of looking at things and yet, at the same time, found themselves trying even harder, almost fanatically, to justify it. This inner turmoil resulting from contradictory impulses, manifesting itself in the dualism of doubt and fanaticism, seems to characterize the moment when projections are ready for withdrawal. According to Marie-Louise von Franz it is these moments or situations without solution, when there is no way out of a conflict, that denote the classical beginning of the process of individuation. It is in experiencing the sense of hopelessness and powerlessness so consistently expressed by men in the mid-life transition, the hopelessness of being pushed and pulled by contradictory impulses, that it becomes clear that a conscious decision, the usual ego function, simply will not suffice. Instead, if a man can muster the courage, accept the prevailing insolubility, and trust in the inner world, the Self is experienced and individuation continues.

Yet two simple words, courage and trust, belie the difficulty of the task, since neither courage nor trust are easy to find at a time of crisis. This is basically because men are conditioned to propel themselves into action and feel that as 'men' they must make a decision, whereas the stance required is that of allowing a process to occur and restraining oneself from consciously interfering with solutions; one needs to learn the art of simply waiting. In the gentle and beautiful words of T.S. Eliot in *East Coker*:

> I said to my soul, be still, and wait without hope
> For hope would be hope for the wrong thing; wait without love
> For love would be love of the wrong thing; there is yet faith
> But the faith and the love and the hope are all in the waiting.

If a man can wait, without interference, then an unfolding of the stages of projection can occur.

From this first stage of seeing aspects of himself — for example his irrationality — only in his wife, a man may move into the stage of experiencing doubt. At this point the object of his projection, for example his wife, may be perceived as behaving inconsistently with the main projected image. Of the following stages, all elaborated by Jung, only the essential points will concern us. These revolve around the observation that, once having recognized that the projection is inconsistent or does not fit the object upon which it has been placed, the individual usually explains it away as an error of judgement. However the next stage is the critical one, since here the individual, not simply satisfied with explaining the inconsistency away as an error, takes it one step further and asks himself where the faulty image could have come from: that is, he says to himself, 'Why did I see that person in the way I did?'. At this stage it is possible to recognize that the source of the 'error' belongs in his own psyche.

This recognition is a profound one in a general sense since it also leads to the recognition and acceptance of the fact that a part of our psyche exists outside our immediate awareness, in short, in our unconscious. I feel this point of recognition is fundamental and indispensable, since it means that a man is recognizing that his unconscious mind is a reality, that the inner world is real, that a psychic reality as such exists. Without this acceptance of a very real inner world, without a man's refusal to dismiss it as sheer imagination, it is most improbable that any progress towards satisfactory resolution of the mid-life crisis could occur. On the surface it seems a fairly straightforward matter to accept that there is an inner world that exerts a powerful influence on our outer life. However I am of the firm conviction that the recognition of such, resulting from asking an honest question about a projection that no longer fits well, is a rare rather than regular phenomenon. A possible explanation lies in the fact that for the first half of their lives males have been heavily conditioned into believing that the conscious mind is the centre of their universe and that the ego in particular is the ruler of this universe.

I find in this modern fixed-belief system that the conscious mind is the centre of the psychological universe, and the ego the ruler of the system — a strange parallel with the ancient view that the earth was the fixed centre of the universe and the sun, planets and stars rotated around it. It is as if man has simply shifted this erroneous belief into the realm of his personal universe. Thus some 400 years after the Copernican revolution we are desperately in need of another revolution that helps man to have a heliocentric understanding of his psyche which will correct the distortion that the ego is the centre of his universe. In many ways Jung can be seen as being to psychology what Copernicus is to astronomy. Jung's theories are systematically based on the view that the conscious mind, the ego, and rational thought are merely a speck in a much vaster psychic universe of which the collective unconscious and the archetypes form a substantial part. In a direct parallel one could consider that the sun, being a symbol of Self according to Jung, is the centre of our psychological planetary system; the ego can then be seen in an analogous sense as the earth. However just as Copernicus was ridiculed and derided, so has Jung attracted much hostility and misunderstanding as exemplified by such descriptions of his work as being nothing other than 'mystical balderdash'. Perhaps man has some basic need to see himself as the centre of the universe whether it be psychological, spiritual or physical, and any attempt to displace him from this position is likely to be met with derision and hostility.

These beliefs lead men to overvalue such egocentric traits as control, precision, rationality, decision-making, objectivity, non-emotionality etc. The thought that there should exist within this egocentric universe an interloper who is capable of influencing their behaviour unawares, is anathema to many men. The possibility of their not being in full control of their behaviour is experienced as an enormous threat and as a total denial of all that constitutes good sense and rational thought. Yet, an ability to ask a serious reflective question about a projection, or a series of projections, is required as the necessary step in withdrawing those parts of ourselves that we have unwittingly placed in others. Hence it is perhaps now clear why I suggested that such a step required courage and above all else a sense of trust that enables one to simply accept that the rational world is but the tip of the iceberg and that below lies a substantial, vast, profound world awaiting discovery. The solely rational approach to the world, with its attendant mechanistic quality, leads to a denial of the inner world and hence an impoverishment of fantasy, feeling, creativity, and imagination . . . these are truly T.S. Eliot's 'hollow men'. In many of the men I interviewed there existed a residual fear of their inner world, or even of the possibility that such a world existed, since its existence posed the threat of rendering their perceived known world unpredictable. Thus the unconscious, and in particular the anima, is experienced as a dangerous threat from within, resulting in a person's inner aspects being once again disowned and projected back onto the world, and the circle of darkness begins anew.

However there is one single but powerful factor that renders it possible that a person may recognize what is projected as being part of himself — this is what Jung calls the 'reflective instinct'. This instinct, which also helps sustain the struggle for recognition, Jung sees as being central to the development of consciousness. Thus he posits that in addition to the basic urges for self-preservation, reproduction and the will to dominate, an additional group of instincts exist which are the drive to activity, the creative instinct and the reflective instinct. Of the latter Jung says:

> The richness of the human psyche and its essential character are probably determined by this reflective instinct. Reflection re-enacts the process of excitation and carries the stimulus over into a series of images which, if the impetus is strong enough, are reproduced in some form of expression.

In essence this reflective instinct can be seen as the urge that drives man to reflect on his experience rather than simply react in a compulsive manner. It frees man from the domination of lower instinctual behaviour and differentiates him from the animal kingdom. With the reflective urge, choice becomes a possibility, but not an inevitability, since it seems that the extent to which this urge to reflect exists varies enormously from individual to individual. However it is this urge, its strength and excitation, that I am firmly convinced differentiates a successful mid-life crisis resolution from an unsuccessful one, since the looking inward, the reflection on the inner world, the formation of images and their expression in such forms as music, drama and writing, all seem to characterize successful resolution. This is simply because the reflective urge and its expression seems to be intrinsically related to the world of the psyche and its development, rather than to the physical world. In the words of M. Esther Harding:

> Individuals in whom the urge to reflect is weak are often content to go through life bounded completely by the limitations of the auto-erotic stage of development. For them the satisfactions of the body suffice; if these fail, they spend their energy in complaining of their ill luck and find a perverted satisfaction in self-pity.

These are the men whom we have previously described as being physically orientated, outside themselves, and distrustful and dismissive towards their own inner world. These are the men who react to the death of the hero of the first half of life by making desperate attempts to resuscitate and keep

119

him alive at all costs. The 'all costs' amounts to a thwarting of the individuation process and the movement towards wholeness, and a failure to experience the mid-life crisis as a creative illness. It seems unequivocal that what characterized the creative illness in the mid-life transitions of Fechner, Freud and Jung was each man's capacity to respond to a reflective urge or instinct. It is in giving expression to this urge that the cultivation of the reflective attitude and the development of consciousness occur.

The reflective attitude can be seen as constituting the mirror that was mentioned in an earlier chapter. This has particular relevance for those men whom I suggested had one side blacked out and hence would receive no reflections of images from the inner world. Now we can see that if the black is removed from the mirror we can receive reflections from our inner world as well as the outer world. Such an analogy reintroduces the anima, since as Emma Jung states: 'One function of the anima is to be a looking glass for a man, to reflect his thoughts, desires and emotions'. By dismissing the anima, the feminine side of his personality, a man is choosing to keep one side of his mirror blacked out and in so doing condemns himself to a half-life, one in which he will be constantly pushed and pulled by the demands of external reality. By reflecting, by allowing the feminine side of himself expression, he can anchor himself in a deeper sense of his being and thus withstand the storms and tempests of outer world demands. This does not mean that he simply withdraws, since this would be a denial of life; rather does it mean that he can increasingly exercise choice over his everyday life and not simply react blindly. It is the failure to reflect, the failure to pause and listen to the inner world, that renders a man highly vulnerable to the external stresses and tensions, since he is literally outside himself, exposed and frightened.

Reflection has a great deal to do with a different and alternative sense of time. 'Outside time' is man-made: clocks, watches, appointments, all geared to external demands which necessitate a pace which is often experienced as being destructively rapid and alienating. 'Inside time' is akin to the seasons, to the plant and *deva* kingdom. One does not expect a flower to come into bloom at 4.35 p.m. or a tree to lose its leaves at precisely 10.15 a.m. Nor can one expect the inner images, feelings, thoughts and intuitions to respond to the demands of one's wristwatch. To be able to experience the reflective urge or process requires a recognition that the inner world of the psyche has a closer relationship to the world of nature than to man-made machines. 'Inside time' may appear ponderously slow and a man's intellect, his ego, will want to shout at him, 'Don't be so stupid, you can't sit all day waiting for an answer'. Hence the conscious pressure will be to disparage an approach that cannot, so to speak, deliver the goods on demand. Yet infuriatingly the inner world, just like nature, is highly independent and unpredictable. Hence we can suddenly experience blinding flashes of intuition; in a sheer fraction of an instant we may grasp a deep understanding of a very complex issue. On such occasions the intellect and rational thought will, of course, want to discredit the understanding on the basis that it is too quick, that there is not sufficient evidence, or that it is 'mere feminine intuition'.

It is as if the conscious mind resists the reflective attitude, and a considerable part of this resistance can be seen as stemming from the marked and almost contrasting sense of time that operates in each realm. Reflection and the reflective attitude are akin to sensing and living one's inner rhythm, imagining we are a flower or tree and awaiting that right moment for movement. To establish this recognition of one's own inner rhythm is a slow, arduous and at times thankless, task. The outer world's demands — those of one's employer, one's family, friends, external organizations, etc. — will all be experienced as pressurizing a man to make a decision, not be so indecisive, and accusing him of 'being an old woman'. To hold on to the feeling of inner rhythm is at times like trying to listen to a beautiful symphony in the middle of a large, noisy, busy city. In many ways it is similar to this, since reflection is the mechanism by which we tune into our 'inner radio'; it is a difficult wave-length to find, easily lost, but once tuned into accurately the sound is superb and it excludes the irrelevancies and static of the outside world. To do so, of course, requires a belief in the existence of the inner world as real and not simply as a figment of one's imagination. In many of the men that I interviewed it became very clear that the reflective instinct was demanding expression, that a powerful pull to reflect on their lives was operating, but more often than not they felt apologetic about it, almost as if to reflect was a form of self-indulgence. This discomfort is indicative of the harsh effect of masculine oppression and conditioning, since I believe that these men, if not most men, feel that to think about themselves is feminine and therefore a sign of weakness. Ironically, within the sense of this book, it *is* feminine, that is, it is anima activity, and as such, a sign of increasing maturity or at least the possibility of it.

The anima, this personification of the feminine aspects of a man's psyche is, as we have so frequently discussed, pressing for expression at this mid point in a man's life, compelled and propelled by the archetypal process of individuation. The anima can then be seen as a mediator between the unconscious and conscious minds. If a man can learn to listen to this aspect of himself he can begin the task of building a relationship between his conscious and unconscious minds and, in so doing, begin the task of removing the accumulated blackness from his inner mirror. Hence we can now see why the first vital step is to recognize those aspects of ourselves that we project onto others – in particular those feminine aspects that a man projects onto women – and to begin the process of re-owning them. It is these aspects, these anima qualities, and receptiveness to the irrational, to intuition and feelings that are the necessary attributes for continuing the movement towards completion and the successful negotiation of the mid-life crisis. The anima then, apart from being the mediator between the two worlds of the unconscious and the conscious, is also that aspect of a man that serves as a guide in negotiating this process.

Nowhere do these functions show up more clearly than in a man's dreams. It is in the world of dreams that many men will experience their first encounter with the anima. Again, in many men, one finds a strong resistance to the world of dreams, and not infrequently a suggestion that a man take note of his dreams is met with a vehement denial that he dreams: 'Oh, I *never* dream', or, 'If I do, it's all just nonsense stuff'. Here we can hear the defensive and derogatory attitude of the rational, conscious mind. Just as reflection is difficult to sustain in a world dedicated to rational thought, control, objectivity and logic, equally difficult is it to accept and listen to the world of dreams. Yet dreams provide us with the most accessible and direct opportunity for reflection. It is in the world of dreams that we can find the compensatory mechanism operating; or, in other words, it is in the world of dreams that we can experience, amongst other things, the opposing and compensatory point of view. I often think of dreams as a sort of party in opposition, opposition not for its own sake (as seems the case with many political parties), but rather in order to present opposing views and previously overlooked points. The aim of such opposition is to produce more complete and just legislation. The conscious mind, and the ego, not unlike the government of the day, can become inflated with their own power and obsessed with maintaining it rather than carrying out the process of democratic government. One does not necessarily have to either believe or accept the opposition viewpoint, nor necessarily act on it, but it is in the interests of justice and wisdom to at least listen to and evaluate it. So is it with the world of dreams: to fully accept this world indiscriminately would be maladaptive, but likewise would it be maladaptive to ignore it completely. We should never forget that we produce our own dreams, they are our productions, and as such we are responsible for them: in this sense alone they warrant listening to.

Yet as already mentioned the masculine ego-consciousness of our contemporary world has a vested interest in discrediting the world of dreams and relegating it to the level of nonsense. 'Nonsense' in terms of logical 'sense' dreams most surely are, since the language of dreams is a symbolic picture-language, a language of its own. But do we assume that a person speaking in a language foreign to us is necessarily speaking nonsense? It is unlikely that this would be the case. Hence it would seem to be the particular nature of the dream world that threatens the conscious masculine ego. Moreover, resistance to this world seems to be intrinsic to mankind: recall, for instance, the response to Joseph and his dreams: 'And Joseph dreamed a dream, and he told it his brethren: and they hated him yet more.'

In this resistance towards dreams one can see a resistance to allowing the feminine aspects to develop, since these, in men, are invariably connected with the world of feeling and irrationality. If a man can accept the reality that he does dream he has very often taken the first step towards developing the feminine aspects of his own being. In recognizing the existence of dreams and then in taking them as a serious cause for reflection, he begins a relationship with his anima, a relationship that will render the 'woman within' a much less troublesome lady. Thus moodiness and irritability may well diminish, since the inner woman will feel at least recognized and not ignored. This does not mean that the process of taking one's fantasies and dreams seriously will not be experienced as painful at times, since it surely will, but it is only by taking them seriously that a man can avoid the inner corruption and decay that are associated with a dead hero. The new hero, or rather new heroic attitude, is to be found in reflecting on the inner world of which the most pronounced form is to be found in one's dreams. As P.W. Martin so profoundly states (in connection with what he terms the constructive technique): 'To realize from experience, that the dream images represent in their own fashion the vital forces at work on the other side of consciousness carries the process the full circle'.

This can be clearly seen in the following dream of a 34-year-old intellectual male in the early stages of a mid-life crisis, who had just commenced a relationship with a female outside his marriage — a relationship in which a strong element of anima projection existed. I will give the dream in full, since it captures in a beautiful way so many of the issues and struggles discussed in this book:

> I went, or was told of a warehouse, by my friend (new female friend) and somehow she was with me showing me the way there. When I arrived I realized that it was now being used for a variety of purposes amongst

which was a used bookshop. I entered this part of the warehouse first and browsed amongst the books, found an interesting collected 18th-19th works of James Hardy, I think, each book was worth 25 cents. Then I noticed C.B. (a very intellectual friend of the dreamer) was next to me, I half jokingly passed an old pamphlet on socialism across to him, he sneeringly scoffed at it, indicating it was a pretty stupid appraisal of socialism.

Somehow my female friend was no longer in the same part of the warehouse, and having discovered I was on the mezzanine floor proceeded to go down to the ground level via what was, or rather appeared to be, a logical opening and stairs down. However the stairs only went half-way down and two women at the desk below warned me, so that I did not fall. Some discussion took place regarding the danger of what was an obvious stairway not in fact being one in a proper sense. Further discussion took place and one or other of the women asked me would I like to see the swimming pool. It was said in such a way to imply that few people saw it and there was some comment about not even my female friend having seen it, although she was familiar with the warehouse. I agreed and the women proceeded up the stairs that had previously been defunct by pulling out a secret extended stairway from underneath which completed the previous partial stairs. Then we all walked around several corners to a lift, pressed buttons and the lift did all the things that lifts do except when the doors opened there wasn't a lift, but stairs leading down. One of the women remarked something to the effect 'that things aren't always what they appear to be'! There was an ever increasing feeling of secrecy on this journey. We went down and down along several dark corridors, like a cellar. Several iron gates, like jail gates, easily opened by leaning against them. Finally, came to a half iron gate, the women continued to lead the way and proceeded through this gate, we were now in a dungeon like area, very damp and very dark and we were walking on planks of some sort. I felt scared, made a noise of some sort and the older of the two women warned me against doing that as it attracted the attention of the rats which she told me were extraordinarily large. Across the way in this very large dark undergound area I noticed several tigers and lions, looked hungry and lean. Journey continued until we came to another part of the dungeon in which there were numerous dogs, jumping up and down, very excitedly. Told they were there to catch the rats. One kept jumping up on me, the woman commanded him to stop, but such demands were only moderately effective. Journeyed a little further and suddenly through the opening of the walls of the dungeon a most beautiful round swimming pool came into view. I remember being stunned and feeling overjoyed by its beauty, superb lush surroundings, tropical palms etc., but above all else the beauty of the light, very very white, compared to the darkness, dampness and musty air we had been in.

Whilst one can appreciate that there is a variety of possible interpretations of this dream, within the context of this book it seems to capture the issues we have been discussing. In particular can one see the role of projection, given this man's outer life situation of a recently formed friendship with a female. It is this friend in the dream who leads him to the warehouse, perhaps a symbol of his psyche. Here he finds himself attracted to books consistent with his outer intellectual orientation, but interestingly enough they are romantic novels that he comes across. There is also the negative contact with an intellectual figure which represents an aspect of himself in the form of his friend 'C.B.'.

The two women represent anima figures and here we can see the vital role of the anima as mediator and guide. She completes the connection between the floors, symbolically the connection between the conscious and unconscious minds. She is also comfortable with things not always being what they appear to be, that is comfortable with the irrational. The remainder of the dream demonstrates the guide qualities of the anima as she leads the man, just as Beatrice led Dante, through the labyrinth of the unconscious as symbolized by cellars and dungeon. The rats, tigers etc.

can be seen as various obstacles in the journey, perhaps negative instincts or destructive tendencies.

Finally the dreamer recalls how he arrived at the beautiful swimming pool, which, consistent with the views offered in this book, can be seen as a symbol of Self. This view is reinforced by the description of the light, a quality that mystics often refer to as being associated with a mystical experience. For example, in an ancient Chinese text on meditation, one of the confirmatory experiences of deep meditation is described as follows:

> At times the following can be experienced: as soon as one is quiet, the light of the eyes begins to blaze up, so that everything before one becomes quite bright as if one were in a cloud.

This dream provides us with a succinct yet comprehensive picture of the role of the anima as a guide in the movement towards completion. For this man, his dream was pointing out, via the anima or female within, that the projection, whilst vital in awakening him to the possibilities, could not lead him any further; that, in this situation, he had to rely on the female within, on his feminine attributes of intuition and acceptance of the inner world. But to do so, as the dream clearly indicates, requires the two conscious attitudes of courage and trust. As Marie-Louise von Franz says in connection with integrating the anima into everyday life: 'We can say that she is generally redeemed by trust, acceptance and love in different variations.'

However dreams are not always as specifically focussed on the anima. Another man, a forty-year-old businessman who had experienced considerable success, followed by a period of collapse and mediocrity, had the following dream during a period of depression and despair:

> I dreamt I was going to buy a new house and was looking over one with a real estate agent. It was a very large white house, beautifully situated on a bluff overlooking the sea from the front and parkland from the rear. However, inside it was in a bad state of repair, rotten floorboards, and much work needed to be done.

If one takes a symbolic view of this dream and sees the house as a symbol of the man himself, then the dream clearly shows his mid-life struggle. It is indicating to him that he needs to do 'much work' on the inside, developing his inner world.

It is in taking his dreams seriously — along with all that the dream world personifies — that a man can give expression to the reflective instinct and develop the reflective attitude that is so vital to the task of the second half of life. This life is sometimes referred to as the symbolic life, since by incorporating our dream world into our everyday life an added dimension is gained, a dimension that transcends the limitations of an ego-embedded life. But this incorporation of our dream world, this reconstruction of the symbolic life, does not come about by simply interpreting our dreams intellectually. Rather must we struggle to understand what the symbols may be conveying to our conscious mind, allow the dream to remain in our consciousness, and explore its possible implications for our everyday life. Too often do people enthusiastically present their dreams to their counsellor along with seemingly brilliant and insightful interpretations, all correct and according to the textbook. The only problem is that their symptoms, behaviour and attitudes remain unchanged. Change, or transformation, does not occur through some magical process of intellectual osmosis. It is sustained and moved by an emotional commitment to self-exploration and understanding. Exploring the implications that our dreams have for our everyday life is a reliable means of bringing about change and facilitating the movement towards integration. For example, the man who dreamed of the house needing major renovations could receive no benefit from this dream if he simply left it at that. He needed to explore what the house meant and what its meaning could be in relation to his present situation. With little effort he realized that it was just like himself at that time, and thus he could begin to explore what aspects within himself needed renovation; he duly arrived at his attitude and behaviour, both of which had been singularly self-destructive. But then the process has to be taken one step further; that is, he needed to ask, 'What in particular in my life is self-destructive, rotten like the floorboards of the house in my dream, and in need of renovation?'. In outer reality it was his inability to take initiative and pursue some interests:

128

he was simply sitting there, quietly rotting away, like the house of his dreams.

A dream can be explored in this way by simply tossing it around in your head, asking such questions as 'I wonder what the dream might be commenting on?', 'What does this woman in my dream mean to me?', 'What sort of person is she?', 'Does the dream have anything to do with my present situation or conflict?'. In general this approach is one of allowing the dream to speak to the conscious mind by cultivating a type of associative intelligence aimed at amplifying the possible association between the dream and a person's everyday life. The difficulty that most men experience when they first approach the dream world is their tendency to hastily dismiss the dream as 'nonsense'. If a man can catch himself dismissing it in this way and can recognize that such an attitude is indicative of a defensive ego-manoeuvre, he will quickly come to realize that such a reaction is further evidence that the dream probably contains some important comments that the ego wants to reject.

Because dreams are often confusing and seemingly meaningless, understanding can be greatly facilitated if an individual has a series of dreams. As Jung states: 'An obscure dream, taken in isolation, can hardly ever be interpreted with any certainty. For this reason I attach little importance to the interpretation of single dreams.' Basic themes and ideas can be more readily recognized and understood if one has several dreams to work on. This can be achieved through the very straightforward means of writing one's dreams down. Not only does this provide a record of the series, but more fundamentally does the act of writing or recording one's dreams have a profound effect on the relationship between the conscious and unconscious aspects of our mind. Writing represents a commitment to one's psychological growth and signifies to the unconscious and the anima in particular that the inner world is being taken seriously, and a type of organic linking-up between consciousness and the unconscious can occur.

This linking can be taken one step further if a record is kept of one's dreams, a dream diary, in which not only the dreams, along with the date of each, are recorded, but space is also left on each page for written attempts at understanding. In this way one can build up a sort of vocabulary of one's own dreams which greatly facilitates understanding. This book is best kept by the bedside since the dreamworld seems unwilling to allow us much time in which to recall a dream. Hence upon waking it is advisable to record whatever one can of a dream even if, initially, that be only one or two words. It ought not be disregarded that paying serious attention to one's dreams seems to be to the psyche what antibodies are to the body. To dismiss one's dreams as trivial is an egocentric act, the consequence of which may well be such regular physical symptoms as hypertension, migraines, nausea and a general state of anxiety. As Jung so clearly states: 'Dreams are the natural reaction of the self-regulating psychic system.' To ignore them is to deny ourselves the opportunity of establishing balance and harmony in our lives, since almost invariably the dreams are a reaction to our conscious attitude and as such provide the necessary warnings and corrections when required.

Another method for approaching the inner world and cultivating the reflective attitude is simply the practice of keeping a diary. Again, like recording dreams, the very act of recording the daily events and in particular the feelings one has experienced during the day, seems to have a self-healing quality. Many men at first react to this suggestion like they do to the suggestion of recording their dreams, that is in a derisive, dismissive manner. However the discipline and practice of keeping a diary, paying particular attention to moods, is a very useful way of developing the inner world. It seems a particularly compatible approach for those men with the writer fantasy since it is entirely consistent with this fantasy and is a means of expressing it. Above all else, a diary provides a man with the possibility of recognizing the patterns in his life: for example, he may come to see over a month that in one particular situation, perhaps a specific meeting, he finds himself feeling tense and reacting angrily. By recognizing the pattern, just as in a series of dreams, the central themes or dilemmas become readily apparent and the problem can be identified — in so doing, a necessary preliminary step towards change has been taken. One of the most regular phenomena I have encountered in counselling is the remarkable incapacity that individuals have to recognize patterns in their own lives. It is as if the failure to see the pattern is intrinsically related to the failure to solve the conflict, since frequently in recognizing the repetitive pattern of our response we experience an inner urgency to change it. Thus a diary, if kept conscientiously, can be of immense value to a man going through a period of conflict. Apart from the invaluable aid it is to recognizing how incredibly repetitive and predictable our moods and behaviour are, the act of keeping a diary is an act of commitment to the reflective life and the inner world. This in itself can greatly assist the inner self-healing or shamanistic components of a man's psyche. If, of course, an individual keeps both a daily diary and a dream diary then the process of reflection and change are greatly enriched. The daily diary, in this connection, apart from bringing the advantages just mentioned, has the distinct advantage of providing a written record of the context and stimuli in the outer world which the inner world of dreams is reacting to or commenting on. Hence understanding can be considerably assisted by keeping a daily diary since it provides the necessary external reference point or mirror-image to the outside world. The combination of a daily diary and dream diary is a perfect example of both sides of the mirror being involved in reflection and in this way one's experience of life is considerably deepened. In this context Jung offers the following advice: 'A dream that is not understood remains a mere occurrence, understood it becomes a living experience'.

A third method of approaching the inner world, one that can be practised solely on its own, or in combination with the diary and dream methods, is that of meditation. Again, as in the other two methods, the essential quality of the meditative process is reflection, looking at and experiencing the inner world as opposed to frantic and frenetic activity in the outer world. If the idea of paying attention to one's dreams and keeping a diary evokes in men a defensive response of derision, then meditation is likely to be perceived as just one further step in the direction of absurdity. In many people's minds, meditation is equated with the occult or black magic. Such misunderstanding reflects fear of the unknown and, considering that meditation has only made its way to the West in relatively recent times, it is not surprising that the word should evoke fear. In its simplest possible form meditation is the practice of sitting quietly and bringing about a certain stillness in one's mind. Too often is it equated with religion, and in particular the mystical religions of the East. Whilst meditation is undoubtedly compatible with religion and religious practice, it is by no means tied to religion. The past decade in the West has witnessed an unprecedented proliferation of meditation teaching centres, of which the most popular has been what is colloquially known as T.M. (transcendental meditation). The physical benefits to be gained from meditation have been substantiated beyond doubt, one of the major ones being the lowering of blood pressure and the consequent reduction in hypertension, the factor invariably associated with cardiac failure.

But apart from bringing about a lowering of the body's actual state of heightened tension and maladaptive preparation for flight or fight, meditation is also known, beyond doubt, to bring about an increase in emotional and mental tranquillity. It is in this connection that it clearly establishes itself as a further way of approaching the inner world. Imagine, by way of analogy, trying to catch a reflection of yourself in a lake or river when the water is muddy or turbulent — obviously a difficult task. So is it with the Self and the inner world: if you are upset, tense, angry or whatever, it is much harder to hear and see yourself, and thus self-awareness is difficult to attain when in a turbulent state. Meditation brings a certain calmness, clearness and stillness to the psyche water in such a way that awareness of Self and the reflections of other aspects of our psyche becomes increasingly possible. It is in the quietness and stillness of meditation that we begin the task of cleansing the inner mirror so that we increasingly come to see and know the inner world of our being and beyond. In the words of the Irish mystic and poet, A.E. (George Russell):

> Meditation is a fiery brooding on that majestical Self.
> We imagine ourselves into Its vastness. We conceive
> ourselves as mirroring Its infinitudes, as moving in
> all things, as living in all beings, in earth, water, air,
> fire, aether.

In this sense it becomes apparent that meditation is a method
aimed at facilitating individuation.

Within this context, given the critical role of the anima in
mid-life, meditation can be seen as an entirely appropriate
anima-initiated activity that is likely to be pursued during
the mid-life crisis. It so clearly reflects anima qualities, in
so far as it is inward-looking, passive, and provides a method
for bridging and mediating the relationship between
consciousness and the unconscious. However, as with all
reflective practices, meditation is not without its dangers,
amongst which is the danger of being preoccupied with
cleansing the inner mirror to the extent that the outer face
of the mirror becomes dull and blackened and consequently
incapable of reflecting the outer world. Such self-absorption
and preoccupation with the inner world is as unhealthy as
an equivalent exclusive preoccupation with the outer world.
Because of the inherent dangers and in the interests of
meditating effectively, men wishing to pursue this method
would be well advised to seek guidance from an accredited
teaching centre or meditation teacher.

If meditation carries the danger of self-absorption and the
loss of the outer reflecting mirror, then the next suggested
method can be considered as substantially more dangerous
in exactly the same way. This is a method developed and
used by Jung himself during his period of intense self-
exploration. He termed the method 'active imagination'.
With this technique Jung suggests that, when referring to
the anima, we put 'direct personal questions to her'. He
argues that practically everyone has the capacity to hold
a conversation with himself, and this technique is precisely
this — a conversation or internal dialogue with oneself.

To have an inner dialogue with oneself has the considerable advantage, akin to the other methods, of taking those
inner aspects of ourselves, particularly the anima, seriously.
Jung pointed out that although people used to proceeding

intellectually and rationally might consider the idea of having a conversation with oneself to be absurd — given the infantile level of their inner world — it is entirely appropriate to treat the anima as an autonomous personality. Further, he declared that 'The more personally she is taken the better'.

In essence then, this method of active imagination means a man holding regular conversations with the inner woman. Upon reflection this may not appear as absurd as it does initially, since most of us can recall saying, at times of crisis, such things as 'What shall I do now?' or 'I wonder how I should proceed?'. In fact internal dialogue is a familiar practice which we do frequently when preparing for some event, interview, meeting etc. One can also observe that young children engage in this activity regularly and indeed it is one of the major mechanisms by which they develop their own sense of self-identity and social skills. It is simply doing it as an adult, and doing it purposely and consciously, that troubles most adults. This resistance to inner dialogue is identical to the resistance to dreams and diaries — it is a characteristically western rational fear of the other side of consciousness. But in practising this technique, as with that of dreams, one is not asked to believe the conversation or the answers from the inner woman. One is simply encouraged to adopt a non-critical attitude so long as the conversation of feelings is proceeding, and then when the discussion has reached an end, to consciously critically evaluate the content as if it were spoken by an outside person.

The obvious advantage of such a technique is that for some men it will be a familiar and comfortable way of dealing with the inner world. In addition, by putting 'direct personal questions to her' as Jung suggests, a man is taking his inner world and anima seriously. This, as we have already seen, is a critical step in approaching and developing the internal world. It requires however a very open mind and, in Jung's view, 'the greatest objectivity and absence of prejudice to give the "other side" the opportunity for perceptible psychic activity'. One means of increasing this objectivity would be to record either in writing or by electronic means, the actual conversation. In fact this inner dialogue may well be an additional method of approaching the inner world for those men who have the writer fantasy. The reason behind this suggestion is that it could be reasonably well argued that creative writing is, in the final analysis, an inner dialogue. This can be perhaps most clearly seen in plays in which dialogue forms the central structure. The inherent danger in such a technique is literally 'going over to the other side' and being invaded by unconscious forces, resulting in mental disturbance. Hence Jung did not advocate wide usage of this technique, and, indeed, an essential condition of use is that the individual have sufficiently strong roots in the outer world and preferably a sympathetic and caring outer companion to share the process with. Tape recording or writing down the dialogue form an important aid against self-absorption in so far as they externalize the conversation, give it objectivity, and render the conversation accessible for critical analysis.

Each of these methods for developing the inner world, the inner woman, and expressing the reflective instinct or urge, will hold varying degrees of attraction for different men. The important task is to ascertain which approach, or combination of approaches, is compatible and comfortable with one's own psyche. But whichever of these methods of mirroring the inner world a man chooses, it is worth bearing in mind that, as Jung pointed out: 'Reflection re-enacts the process of excitation and carries the stimulus over into a series of images, which, if the impetus is strong enough are reproduced in some form of expression'. It is the 'some form of expression' that forms the additional task. This involves the creative instinct and would lead a man to consider varying ways of giving actual outer expression to the inner images and feelings that one encounters via the reflective process. This may take the form of such traditional activities as art, sculpture, music, writing, drama or any other form of creative activity. The desire to engage in creative activity was a prevalent theme amongst the men I interviewed. As previously mentioned, most of them, when asked was there anything they wished they could do, mentioned some creative activity such as painting or playing a musical instrument. Hence these thoughts can now be seen as being entirely appropriate at the mid-life point since they are the means of giving expression to the mirror images that are being stirred and encountered at this stage. But as with their reaction to most other aspects of the inner world, men have to overcome their own prejudice against these thoughts. They have to overcome their fear of being thought silly or childish, and to recognize that pursuing such interests may well be a step towards completion. It is irrelevant what a man chooses to do; what is critical is that he answers the inner prompting and finds a method of expression that allows him to take his inner world seriously. It is in turning inwards, in reflecting, in building a relationship with the inner woman, that a man can turn his mid-life crisis into a creative illness that he cures by developing the shaman within. In these circumstances the mid-life crisis is truly an initiatory illness, initiating man into true adulthood where real choice, based on a knowledge of oneself, can be made. This knowledge is of the kind which uses both sides of the mirror, the inner and outer reflections, and not simply the reflections of outer demands and values.

If this book has one central theme then it has been that of the reality of the inner world and the importance of taking it seriously in the second half of life. In the words of Saint Augustine:

> Seek not abroad, turn back into thyself,
> for in the inner man dwells the truth.

Endnotes

1   Others have been there before!
Page
13   John Milton, *Paradise Lost,* Book IV.
14   A. P. Tchekov, *Ivanov,* Everyman's Library No. 941 (Dent).
15   Eliot Jaques, 'Death and the Mid-Life Crisis' in *International Journal of Psychoanalysis* 46 (1965), pp. 504–14.
15   T. S. Eliot, *East Coker* (Faber & Faber, London, 1941).
16   T. S. Eliot, *The Dry Salvages* (Faber & Faber, London, 1941).
16   T. S. Eliot, *Collected Poems 1909-1935* (Faber & Faber, London, 1951).
17   C. G. Jung, 'Marriage as a Psychological Relationship', in *C.W.* vol. 17 (Routledge & Kegan Paul, London, 1954), p. 193.
     [Throughout these notes, *'C.W.'* refers to *The Collected Works of C. G. Jung.*]
18   T. S. Eliot, *op. cit.*
18   Emma Jung, *Animus and Anima* (Spring Publications, 1978), p. 67.
19   Marie-Louise von Franz, *C. G. Jung: His Myth in our Time* (Little Brown & Co., 1975), p. 105.
19   C. G. Jung, 'The Stages of Life' in *C.W.* vol. 8 (Routledge & Kegan Paul, London, 1960), p. 399.
19   H. Ellenberger, *The Discovery of the Unconscious* (Basic Books, New York, 1970).
20   Eliot Jaques, *op. cit.*
20   Erik Erikson, *Childhood and Society* (Norton & Co., New York, 1950).
21   Walter Lowrie (ed.), *Gustav Theodore Fechner, Religion of a Scientist* (Pantheon Books, New York, 1946), pp. 36–42.
23   H. Ellenberger, *op. cit.,* pp. 444–9.
24   *ibid,* p. 447.
25   C. G. Jung, 'The Soul and Death' in *C.W.* vol. 8.
25   A. Jaffe (ed.), *Memories, Dreams, Reflections of C. G. Jung* (Routledge & Kegan Paul, London, 1963).
26   *ibid,* p. 173.
27   Marie-Louise von Franz, *op. cit.,* p. 109.
28   Erwin H. Ackcrknecht, 'Problems of Primitive Medicine' in

Bulletin of the History of Medicine XI, no. 5 (1942), pp. 503–21.

28   Quoted in Ellenberger, *op. cit.,* p. 39, from George Nioradze, 'Der Schamanismus bei den sibirischen Volkern' (Strecken & Schroder, Stuttgart, 1925).

30   C. G. Jung, 'The Stages of Life' in *C.W.* vol. 8, p. 399.

2   The social context
Page

34   Poems of W. B. Yeats (Macmillan Education, 1962), p. 177.

3   The individual context

36   D. B. Bromley, *The Psychology of Human Ageing* (Pelican).

42   Frances Wickes, *The Inner World of Choice* (Prentice-Hall, New Jersey, 1963), p. 61.

42   Poems of W. B. Yeats, *op. cit.,* p. 66.

4   The family context

43   Erik Erikson, *op. cit.*

47   C. G. Jung, 'On the Psychology of the Unconscious' in *C.W.* vol. 7 (Routledge & Kegan Paul, London, 1966), p. 75.

48   Eliot Jaques, *op. cit.*

48   Sigmund Freud, 'Thoughts for the times on war and death', Standard Edition 14 (Hogarth Press, 1915).

5   The occupational context

50   Erik Erikson, 'Identity and the Life Cycle' in *Psychological Issues* vol. 1, no. 1 (1959), p. 92.

53   Karl Marx, *1844 Manuscripts* (ed. Dirk J. Struik, Lawrence & Wishart, 1970), p. 110.

55   Peter Marris, *Loss and Change* (Routledge & Kegan Paul, London, 1974), p. 26.

56   *ibid,* p. 31.

58   Geoffrey Gorer, *Death, Grief and Mourning in Contemporary Britain* (Cresser Press, London, 1965).

58   C. G. Jung, 'The Soul and Death' in *C.W.* vol. 8, p. 407.

64   Erik Erikson, *op. cit.,* p. 91.

6 Marriage and the mid-life crisis

Page

72 C. G. Jung, 'Marriage as a Psychological Relationship' in *C.W.* vol. 17, p. 193.

74 *ibid,* p. 194.

77 Emma Jung, *op. cit.,* p. 26.

78 Gail Sheehy, *Passages* (Bantam Books, 1977), p. 353.

7 Summary and overview of the crisis

86 Søren Kierkegaard, *Sickness Unto Death* (tr. Walter Lowrie, Princeton, 1941).

88 Alexei Tolstoy, *Memoirs of a Madman* (tr. A. Maude, World Classics), pp. 210ff.

88 W. Y. Evans-Wentz, *Tibetan Yoga and Secret Doctrines,* The Supreme Path of Discipleship, Book 1 (London, 1935), p. 85.

89 H. Ellenberger, *op. cit.,* p. 447.

89 Mircea Eliade, *Yoga Immortality and Freedom* (tr. W. Trask, Routledge & Kegan Paul, London, 1958), p. 323.

90 T. S. Eliot, *Little Gidding* (Faber & Faber, London, 1942).

8 The Self and the anima

92 C. G. Jung, 'The Structure and Dynamics of the Psyche' in *C.W.* vol. 8, p. 394.

93 C. G. Jung (ed.), *Man and His Symbols* (Aldus Books, London, 1964).

94 C. G. Jung, 'Unconscious and Individuation' in *C.W.* vol. 9, part I (Routledge & Kegan Paul, London, 1959), p. 275.

95 C. G. Jung, 'Psychology and Alchemy' in *C.W.* vol. 12 (Routledge & Kegan Paul, London, 1953), p. 41.

95 Marie-Louise von Franz, *op. cit.,* pp. 73-4.

95 *ibid,* p. 74.

95 C. G. Jung, 'Forewords to White's "God and the Unconscious"' in *C.W.* vol. II (Routledge & Kegan Paul, London, 1958), p. 307.

96 Emma Jung, *op. cit.,* p. 79.

97 C. G. Jung, 'The Structure and Dynamics of the Psyche' in *C.W.* vol. 8, p. 158.

98 E. A. Bennett, *What Jung Really Said* (Schocken Books, New York, 1967), p. 154.

99   C. G. Jung, 'Marriage as a Psychological Relationship' in *C.W.* vol. 17, p. 198.

100   Anthony Storr, *Jung* (ed. F. Kermode, Fontana, 1973), p. 51.

102   C. G. Jung, *Aion, C.W.* vol. 9, part 2 (2nd ed., Routledge & Kegan Paul, London, 1968), p. 268.

106   Marie-Louise von Franz, *Interpretation of Fairy Tales* (Spring Publications, 1978), p. 63.

106   Anthony Storr, *op. cit.,* p. 51.

108   Frances G. Wickes, *The Inner World of Choice* (Prentice-Hall, 1976), p. 183.

108   *ibid,* p. 188.

109   Emma Jung, *op. cit.,* p. 81.

110   E. R. Dodds, *The Greeks and the Irrational* (Univ. of California Press, 1973), p. 80.

111   W. B. Yeats (ed.), *Fairy and Folk Tales of Ireland* (Colin Smythe, 1973), p. 385.

112   Marie-Louise von Franz, 'The Process of Individuation' in *Man and his Symbols, op. cit.,* p. 188.

9 Approaching the inner world
Page

115   Oscar Wilde, *Selected Essays and Poems* (Penguin, 1954), p. 49.

115   Marie-Louise von Franz, *Interpretation of Fairy Tales, op. cit.,* p. 69.

116   T. S. Eliot, *East Coker* (Faber & Faber, 1941).

116   C. G. Jung, 'The Spirit Mercurius' in *C.W.* vol. 13 (Routledge & Kegan Paul, London, 1967), pp. 199–200.

118   C. G. Jung, 'The Structure and Dynamics of the Psyche' in *C.W.* vol. 8, pp. 117–18.

119   *ibid.*

119   M. Esther Harding, *Psychic Energy: Its Source and Transformation* (Princeton Univ. Press, 1973), p. 31.

120   Emma Jung, *op. cit.,* p. 65.

124   Genesis, chapter 37, verse 5.

124   P. W. Martin, *Experiment in Depth* (Routledge & Kegan Paul, London, 1955), p. 37.
     In quoting this dream, no corrections of grammar have been made. It was recorded by the dreamer.

127   *The Secret of the Golden Flower* (tr. Richard Wilhelm, Routledge & Kegan Paul, London, 1975), p. 50.

127   Marie-Louise von Franz, *op. cit.,* p. 62.

129   C. G. Jung, 'Practical Use of Dream Analysis' in *The Practice*

of *Psychotherapy, C.W.* vol. 16 (Routledge & Kegan Paul, London, 1954), p. 150.

130   C. G. Jung, *Analytical Psychology: Its Theory and Practice,* The Tavistock Lectures (Routledge & Kegan Paul, London, 1968), p. 124.

131   C. G. Jung, 'Fundamental Questions of Psychotherapy' in *The Practice of Psychotherapy, C.W.* vol. 16, p. 123.

133   A.E., *The Candle of Vision* (Macmillan, London, 1919).

133   C. G. Jung, 'Anima and Animus' in *Two Essays on Analytical Psychology, C.W.* vol. 7, pp. 200–1.

134   *ibid.,* p. 202.

135   C. G. Jung, *C.W.* vol. 8, pp. 117–18.

136   *De Vera Religione,* chapter 39, para. 72.

Index